Philosophy of
Media Sounds

edited by Michael Schmidt

Philosophy of
Media Sounds

ATROPOS PRESS

CONTENTS

Prelude to a Philosophy of Media Sounds
Michael Schmidt

The Art-Work of the Future / IV. Outlines of the Artwork of the Future
Richard Wagner

The Work of Art in the Age of Mechanical Reproduction
Walter Benjamin

The Radio Symphony: An Experiment in Theory
Theodor W. Adorno

The Grain of the Voice
Roland Barthes

The Phonograph: The Toy that Shrank the National Chest
Marshall Mcluhan

The Future of Music
John Cage

A Thousand Plateaus / Excerpt from "1837: Of the Refrain"
Gilles Deleuze & Felix Guattari

Prelude to a Philosophy of Media Sounds
by Michael Schmidt

One of the earliest descriptions of the effect that the technical preservation and reproduction of music has on the listener can be found in Thomas Mann's "Zauberberg" (Magic Mountain). For the narrator, the pleasure of music is closely related to the addiction of the gambler: "What achievement... was it that delivered our friend from his card-tic and drove him to another, nobler but by no means less peculiar passion? It was a flowing cornucopia of a serene and soulful pleasure. It was a music machine. It was a gramophone."

It is the broadcasting and recording media which has made the music of all epochs and styles omniavailable and omnipresent:"the tape recorder in combination with longplay-record revolutionized the repertory of classical music. Just as the tape meant a new study of spoken rather than written languages, so it brought in the entire musical culture of many centuries and countries. Where before there had been a narrow selection from periods and composers, the tape recorder, combined with the longplay record, gave a full musical spectrum that made the sixteenth century as available as the nineteenth, and Chinese folk songs as accessible as the Hungarian" (Herbert Marshall McLuhan: Understanding Media). It is due to records, compact-discs, cassette-recorders, walkmen, radio and television that music is not only universally available but has also became a universal presence. Whether department store, restaurant, train station or airport, music has become a constant companion of our everyday life.

Has music, by its media-caused omnipresence, approached the murmuring drone from which it may once have sprung – is music once again close to the murmuring of water and wind, those omnipresent sounds of nature? Or is it rather that mass media has made music a part of the noise which is characteristic of our technical world, whose machines and acoustic signals drown out nature altogether, making it inaudible? What has happened to music, to its expression and to its meaning in the age of electronic media?

Sound wallpapers

When in 1933 Joseph Goebbels, the Nazi propaganda minister responsible for the German broadcasting corporation gave a speech on the occasion of the Berlin radio exposition, he declared the new medium to be a "Großmacht" (a superpower). Although the first radio program had only been broadcast a decade earlier, radio had already become a mass medium with a national, indeed world-wide range and millions of radio sets to receive its programs. The mass distribution of radio sets gave the Nazi government the opportunity to initiate a dramaturgically clever programme plan which helped to shape public opinion according to Nazi aesthetic and political ideology. In the Weimar Republic, when the new medium was built up as "Unterhaltungsrundfunk" (entertainment radio), music had already become the epitome of media art. Music, unlike any other programformat, turned out to be perfectly suited to entertain the listener, to provide for his distraction and relaxation; in short, to cheer up the soul of the people, especially when the political and later military situation became gloomy. In the Third Reich the indulgence of political propaganda was balanced by an extensive musical program designed to influence the listener's feelings in the party's favor and simultaneously veil the fact that he or she was under the influence of the Nazi-slogans.

On March 25, 1933, when the radio directors had their first meeting, Joseph Goebbels gave a speech outlining this plan in detail: "Anything but dullness. Anything but monotony. Anything but displaying our views. Anything but the idea, that one can best serve the National Socialist government by broadcasting bellowing marches evening after evening... The radio should never suffer from its intention. People feel the intention and they are put out." Before any other broadcast the "Wunschkonzert für die Wehrmacht" (the listener's choice program for the army) became the prototype of Nazi program planning in the broadcasting corporation of the Third Reich, the "Reichsrundfunk". Exactly one month after the beginning of World War Two this popular sunday afternoon broadcast began to lure almost half the German population to their radio sets – week after week. While the towns of the "Großdeutsche Reich" (Greater German Empire) turned more and more into expanses of rubble, while millions and millions were killed in the concentration camps and in the war, the german radio stations broadcasted merry tunes: Schlager (hits), operettas, popular film music, sometimes even the officially banned swing sound. While German media of today are not controlled by a criminal government like the Nazi regime, music is still used as a constant stream of background entertainment, serving in the manipulation and emotional charge of consumer-shopping-malls (e.g. Muzak), advertising and the news, which, as a result, mutated into news-shows.

From *mousike* to collage

Originally the Greek concept of *mousike* combined poetry, dance and music in a single work related through rhythm and offered by the muses. The myth of Orpheus tells us about the magical power of music: the song and the lyre vanquish men and animals. For Pythagoras and his school, music most obviously confirms the universal harmony of the cosmos which, just like musical consonances, is the function of a numerical ratio. Plato emphasized the moral effect of the *mousike*, its ability to strengthen the veil and to threaten human morality. He condemned the music of mere pleasure and asked for a moral music (*The Republic*). For Aristotle, too, the first task of music was the formation of moral character by way of musical imitation. Moreover, he emphasized the cathartic quality of music, its healing purification of all passions, and he appreciated it as an activity without a specific purpose, as a pleasure and a game. Music, for Aristotle, was also a 'poietic', which is to say a work that produces practical knowledge. Before 1800, the Aristotelian doctrine of art as imitation of nature was fundamental to both artistic creation and evaluation. Elaborating on the mimetic theory, the doctrine of the Affections related music to rhetoric. It was thought that music could imitate both animate and inanimate nature, the inflections of speech, and the emotions. This imitation was accomplished by rhetorical method, and its aim was to arouse the listener's consciousness.

Arthur Schopenhauer's metaphysics describes a world with two basic components: a system of eternal ideas and an unquiet will. For him, the arts other than music symbolize the ideas, but only music reveals the will, which is the more fundamental of the two. Schopenhauer described music in *The World as Will and Representation* (§52) as the immediate objectification of the will, ". . . music does not express this or that particular and definite pleasure, this or that affliction, pain, sorrow, horror, gaiety, merriment, or peace of mind, but joy, pain, sorrow, horror, gaiety, merriment, peace of mind *themselves*, to a certain extent in the abstract, their essential nature, without any accessories, and so also without the motives for them." Schopenhauer thus assigned to music a deeper cognitive meaning than any other philosopher before. Music was now no imitation of nature but rather an incarnation of nature.

When, in 1877, Thomas Edison applied for a patent on his phonograph, the pioneering step in the development of sound recording was taken. Up to this time recordings of Occidental music were confined to their "logos", i.e., to a musical notation of its rational structures. Only the phonograph offered the possibility to record and reproduce the sensual, random and material aspects of music which are beyond any written notation. Then, unlike the phonograph's mechanical recording of voice and sound the electromagnetic sound recording of the tape recorder could manipulate the recorded material by way of cut, montage and filter. Finally digital sound recording cleared recorded material of even more all limitations caused by recording and broadcast media. Thus, the sound of acoustic material could be reproduced authentically, for the-first time.

The musical work of art is only complete when performed. But performance is dependent on a certain place and time. Mechanical sound recording freed music from its performance conditions. Every musical act used to be a unique, separate, unrepeatable event. With electromagnetic recording technology music was no longer dependent on a unique concert-performance. Manipulations of recorded material, such as the collages of several performances, created sonic results no single performance could ever produce. In spite of the high-tech facilities that offer the possibilities to record, reproduce and manipulate sound, there was an audible gap between the performance and its recording, which has been eliminated by today's more sophisticated digital sound recording. Thus the auditory difference between reality and simulation disappeared altogether.

The "pre-digital" broadcasting and recording media took music out of its traditional context and established the non-musical sound in music. Pierre Schaeffer, for example, born in Nancy, France, in 1910, is one of the pioneers of *musique concrète*, which allied itself to the new media techniques. In 1948 Mr. Schaeffer, who called himself a composer, theoretician, broadcasting engineer, writer, sound researcher and teacher, began hunting for sounds of everyday life to capture them on a tape machine, arranging them in complex sound compositions. Mr. Schaeffer's *Musique Concrète* inspired many modern composers, such as Karlheinz Stockhausen, to work with electro-acoustics. Microphone, loudspeaker and amplifier, as well as the electric guitar, made the body audible, particularly in rock music. "Roughness, *le grain,* is the body of the singing voice", says Roland Barthes in his essay "The Grain of the Voice". The microphone gave the roughness of the voice back to an Occidental music characterized until then by its discursive forms. The electric guitar modulations created by the slightest twitch of the finger brought back the roughness of the instrumental sound. It was a come-back of everything Occidental music had successfully abolished in its scores, instruments and instrumentalized voices: the come-back of the non-musical sound, of all things transitory, spontaneous and physical.

Digital recording bridged the auditory gap between the reality of musical performance and its simulation on, say, compact disc, so perfectly that it created a musical hyperroom, with the inherent potential of all possible acoustics - the one already realized as well the one to come. The postmodern composer or the Rap musician takes this musical media produced hyperreality into account by using anything and everything - style copies as veil as direct quotations or digital samples of existing recordings and other ready made sounds coming his way by using only acoustic things as material for his musical collages.

Sound games

"The first technician of music was the first to stop being a good musician," wrote Theodor W. Adorno in an essay entitled "Musik und Technik", commenting on the symphonist Hector Berlioz. Adorno accuses Berlioz - as well as his successors Franz Liszt and Richard Strauss - of having transformed the "negation of meaning into meaning" - by means of "technification" and "technique of surprise".

In the "Symphonie Fantastique" Berlioz applies this "technique of surprise," by extending the instrumentation of the orchestral sound (e.g. real church bells are used in the "Dies Irae"). But for Adorno a style of composing that manipulates its musical material only in a technical sense risks losing its musical content to the advantage of a technical virtuosity producing mere musical effects. Ever since Hector Berlioz' "Symphonie Fantastique" dating from 1820 the arrangement of "shocks" by a "technification" of the aesthetic material coincides, according to Adorno's essay "Klangfiguren", with a loss of subjectivity and an increased "alienation from self" in art (in English the German word "Technik" has the double sense of technique and technology). It is in fact true that Berlioz' music concedes a central role to the "imprevu", that is, the unforeseen and, in terms of the inherent musical logic, the "unforeheard" as it were.

Adorno labeled modernism as a painful, intrinsic movement of musical material by someone desperately composing in a time devoid of all meaning - Arnold Schoenberg's serial music comes to mind. In his essay "Schoenberg and Progress" Adorno claimed, "the inhumanity of art has to outperform that of the world for the sake of humanity . . . Out of the veil known for something that has never existed, the technique of art achieves its seriousness. It is all the more nowadays, as the attention intrinsic to the consistency of art technique constitutes the very content of a work of art. The shocks of the incomprehensible caused by art technique in a time devoid of all meaning become the opposite. They illuminate a meaningless world. Modern music sacrifices itself to this. It burdens itself with a deep sense of guilt, with all the darkness of the world. To recognize misfortune is its happiness; to refrain from the mere illusion of beauty is its beauty." This is no longer true for the postmodern composer who loves playing games in a musical hyperroom. He keeps arranging his samples or his musical filing cards. Everything is ready and waiting. "Gimme two records and I'll make you a universe," says avantgarde-DJ "Spooky" (*Songs of a Dead Dreamer*, 1996). Compared with

Adorno's gloomy ethic-aesthetic dictum, composer and performer John Zorn's poetological reflections seem more like a *Froehliche Wissenschaft* (a "gay science" in the sense of Nietzsche) of music and media: "I grew up in New York City as a media freak, watching movies and TV and buying hundreds of records. There's also a lot of jazz in me, but there's also a lot of rock, a lot of classical, a lot of ethnic music, a lot of movie sound-moments, in disparate sound blocks, I sometimes find it convenient to store these "events" on filing cards so they can be sorted and ordered with minimum effort. (John Zorn *Spillane*, 1987). DJ Spooky creates musical collages by using the sampling-technique. He writes in the booklet of his CD-Album "Necropolis: The Dialog Project", "The mix: a fusion of different meanings whose previous connotations have been corralled into a space where they are so placed that differences in time, space, and culture are collapsed within the immediate realm of the telepological present... The word phonograph simply means 'writing sound'. See the record as a device that allows the mnemonic construction of a paraspace where all is flux, and the only constant is change... In a prismatic fashion through the union of form and content, the DJ refracts meaning from the dense locale of culture and places the rays of meaning, in a rhizomatic fashion, back in their original locale, the human mind. This refraction of meaning leads one from the singular to the plural, and in the process opens the ego-centric self to the spaces of the multiple where all things are linked."

Flowing cornucopia

What has happened to music, to its expression, and to its meaning, in the age of media? In his essay "Media Aesthetics in Europe", philosopher Wolfgang Schirmacher writes, "in media we write our autobiography . . . 'express yourself' is the advice of the media icon Madonna, and don't ask for permission . . . the difference between real and simulation has disappeared. The distinction between the original and the reproduction has become meaningless . . . media in all forms and with any kind of message are merely material for a personal collage (Wagner's Gesamtkunstwerk on a small scale)." This is true. "I consider the mixes created by a DJ to be mood sculptures" (DJ Spooky). This is also true. But it is due to today's media that music is not only universally available, for musical collages for example, but has also become a universal presence, turned into a *musique d'ammeublement,* as the composer Satie put it, which we cannot avoid, and which we do not listen to, but simply hear.

Curiously enough the rest (a silent pause) is one of the most powerful elements in music. Haydn added a long rest at the end of his "Joke" quartet, to give the false impression that the work was over when in fact there was still two bars to play. A rest can obscure any sense of what is coming next. The American composer John Cage took the rest to its extreme with his completely silent piece 4'33''. The instructions on the score are to play nothing at all for exactly four minutes and thirty-three seconds. The "music" thus consists of any sounds made by the audience or the traffic outside.

Richard Wagner's *Rheingold* prelude begins with an E flat-major triad in the basses and then strides across the overtones of its root-note E-flat without developing melodically or even thematically. Shortly before the invention of the phonograph this music already approaches a murmuring drone state, leaving behind the discourse of musical speech, its vocabulary, or significations, and thus becomes a flowing cornucopia of no specific fare but with the inherent potentiality of all forms—just like the Rhine that keeps flowing with a murmuring drone.   Media opened music to sound, and made it universally available material for personal collages. At the same time media puts music in the state of a constant murmuring drone, an incessant flowing.

The Art-Work of the Future / IV. Outlines of the Artwork of the Future
by Richard Wagner
Translated by William Ashton Ellis

If we consider the relation of modern art—so far as it is truly Art—to public life, we shall recognise at once its complete inability to affect this public life in the sense of its own noblest endeavour. The reason hereof is, that our modern art is a mere product of Culture and has not sprung from Life itself; therefore, being nothing but a hot-house plant, it cannot strike root in the natural soil, or flourish in the natural climate of the present. Art has become the private property of an artist-caste; its taste it offers to those alone who *understand* it; and for its understanding it demands a special study, aloof from actual life, the study of *art-learning.* This study, and the understanding to be attained thereby, each individual who has acquired the gold wherewith to pay the proffered delicacies of art conceives to-day that he has made his own: if, however, we were to ask the Artist whether the great majority of art's amateurs are able to understand him in his best endeavours, he could only answer with a deep-drawn sigh. But if he ponder on the infinitely greater mass of those who are perforce shut out on every side by the evils of our present social system from both the understanding and the tasting of the sweets of modern art, then must the artist of to-day grow conscious that his whole art-doings are, at bottom, but an egoistic, self-concerning business; that his art, in the light of public life, is nothing else than luxury and superfluity, a self-amusing pastime. The daily emphasised, and bitterly deplored abyss between so-called culture and un-culture is so enormous; a bridge between the two so inconceivable; a reconcilement so impossible; that, had it any candour, our modern art, which grounds itself on this unnatural culture, would be forced to admit, to its deepest shame, that it owes its existence to a life-element which in turn can only base *its* own existence on the utter dearth of culture among the real masses of mankind.

The only thing which, in the position thus assigned to her, our Modern Art should be able to effect—and among honest folk, indeed, endeavours—namely, *the spreading abroad of culture*, she cannot do; and simply for the reason that, for Art to operate on Life, she must be herself the blossom of a natural culture, i.e., such an one as has grown up from below, for she can never hope to rain down culture from *above*. Therefore, taken at its best, our "cultured" art resembles an orator who should seek to address himself in a foreign tongue to a people which does not understand it: his highest flights of rhetoric can only lead to the most absurd misunderstandings and confusion.—

Let us first attempt to trace the theoretic path upon which Modern Art must march forward to redemption from her present lonely, misprised station, and toward the widest understanding of general public Life. That this redemption can only become possible by the *practical* intermediation of public Life, will then appear self-evident.

****

We have seen that *Plastic Art* can only attain creative strength by going to her work in unison with *artistic* Man, and not with men who purpose mere *utility*.

Artistic Man can only fully content himself by uniting every branch of Art into the *common* Artwork: in every segregation of his artistic faculties he is unfree, not fully that which he has power to be; whereas in the common Artwork he is *free*, and fully that which he has power to be.

The *true* endeavour of Art is therefore all-embracing: each unit who is inspired with a true *art-instinct* develops to the highest his own particular faculties, not for the glory of these special faculties, but for the glory of *general Manhood* in Art.

The highest conjoint work of art is the Drama: it can only be at hand in all its possible fulness, when in it each *separate branch of art* is at hand in *its own utmost fulness*.

The true Drama is only conceivable as proceeding from a *common urgence of every art* towards the most direct appeal to a *common public*. In this Drama, each separate art can only bare its utmost secret to their common public through a mutual parleying with the other arts; for the purpose of each separate branch of art can only be fully attained by the reciprocal agreement and co-operation of all the branches in their common message.

Architecture can set before herself no higher task than to frame for a fellowship of artists, who in their own persons portray the life of Man, the special surroundings necessary for the display of the Human Artwork. Only that edifice is built according to Necessity, which answers most befittingly an aim of man: the highest aim of man is the artistic aim; the highest artistic aim—the Drama. In buildings reared for daily use, the builder has only to answer to the lowest aim of men: beauty is therein a luxury. In buildings reared for luxury, he has to satisfy an unnecessary and unnatural need: his fashioning therefore is capricious, unproductive, and unlovely. On the other hand, in the construction of that edifice whose every part shall answer to a common and artistic aim alone,—thus in the building of the *Theatre*, the master-builder needs only to comport himself as *artist*, to keep a single eye upon the *art-work*. In a perfect theatrical edifice, Art's need alone gives law and measure, down even to the smallest detail. This need is twofold, that of giving and that of *receiving*, which reciprocally pervade and condition one another. The Scene has firstly to comply with all the conditions of "space" imposed by the joint (*gemeinsam*) dramatic action to be displayed thereon: but secondly, it has to fulfil those conditions in the sense of bringing this dramatic action to the eye and ear of the spectator in intelligible fashion. In the arrangement of the *space for the spectators*, the need for optic and acoustic understanding of the artwork will give the necessary law, which can only be observed by a union of beauty and fitness in the proportions; for the demand of the collective (*gemeinsam*) audience is the demand for the artwork, to whose comprehension it must be distinctly led by everything that meets the eye. (1) Thus the spectator transplants himself upon the stage, by means of all his visual and aural faculties; while the performer becomes an artist only by complete absorption into the public. Everything, that breathes and moves upon the stage, thus breathes and moves alone from eloquent desire to impart, to be seen and heard within those walls which, however circumscribed their space, seem to the actor from his scenic standpoint to embrace the whole of humankind; whereas the public, that representative of daily life, forgets the confines of the auditorium, and lives and breathes now only in the artwork which seems to it as Life itself, and on the stage which seems the wide expanse of the whole World.

Such marvels blossom from the fabric of the Architect, to such enchantments can he give a solid base, when he takes the purpose of the highest human artwork for his own, when he summons forth the terms of its enlivening from the individual resources of his art. On the other hand, how rigid, cold, and dead does his handiwork appear when, without a higher helpmeet than the aim of luxury, without the artistic necessity which leads him, in the Theatre, to invent and range each detail with the greatest sense of fitness, he is forced to follow every speculative whim of his self-glorifying caprice; to heap his masses and trick out his ornament, in order to stereotype to-day the vanity of some boastful plutocrat, to-morrow the honours of a modernised Jehovah!

But not the fairest form, the richest masonry, can alone suffice the Dramatic Artwork for the perfectly befitting spacial terms of its appearance. The Scene which is to mount the picture of Human Life must, for a thorough understanding of this life, have power to also show the lively counterfeit of Nature, in which alone artistic Man can render up a speaking likeness of himself. The casings of this Scene, which look down chill and vacantly upon the artist and the public, must deck themselves with the fresh tints of Nature, with the warm light of heaven's æther, to be worthy to take their share in the human artwork. Plastic Architecture here feels her bounds, her own unfreedom, and casts herself, athirst for love, into the arms of Painting, who shall work out her redemption into fairest Nature.

Here *Landscape-painting* enters, summoned by a common need which she alone can satisfy. What the painter's expert eye has seen in Nature, what he now, as artist, would fain display for the artistic pleasure of the full community, he dovetails into the united work of all the arts, as his own abundant share. Through him the scene takes on complete artistic truth: his drawing, his colour, his glowing breadths of light, compel Dame Nature to serve the highest claims of Art. That which the landscape-painter, in his struggle to impart what he had seen and fathomed, had erstwhile forced into the narrow frames of panel-pictures,—what he had hung up on the egoist's secluded chamber-walls, or had made away to the inconsequent, distracting medley of a picture-barn,—*therewith* will he henceforth fill the ample framework of the Tragic stage, calling the whole expanse of scene as witness to his power of recreating Nature. The illusion which his brush and finest blend of colours could only hint at, could only distantly approach, he will here bring to its consummation by artistic practice of every known device of optics, by use of all the art of 'lighting. The apparent roughness of his tools, the seeming grotesqueness of the method of so-called 'scene-painting,' will not offend him; for he will reflect that even 'the finest camel's-hair brush is but a humiliating instrument, when compared with the perfect Artwork; and the artist has no right to *pride* until he is *free, i.e.*, until his artwork is completed and alive, and he, with all his helping tools, has been absorbed into it. But the finished artwork that greets him from the stage will, set within this frame and held before the common gaze of full publicity, immeasurably more content him than did his earlier work, accomplished with more delicate tools. He will not, forsooth, repent the right to use this scenic space to the benefit of such an artwork, for sake of his earlier disposition of a flat-laid scrap of canvas! For as, at the very worst, his work remains the same no matter what the frame from which it looks, provided only it bring its subject to intelligible show: so will his artwork, in *this* framing, at any rate effect a livelier impression, a greater and more universal understanding, than the whilom landscape picture.

The organ for all understanding of Nature, is Man: the landscape-painter had not only to impart to men this understanding, but to make it for the first time plain to them by depicting Man in the midst of Nature. Now by setting his artwork in the frame of the Tragic stage, he will expand the individual man, to whom he would address himself, to the associate manhood of full publicity, and reap the satisfaction of having spread his understanding out to that, and made it partner in his joy. But he cannot fully bring about this public understanding until he allies his work to a joint and all-intelligible aim of loftiest Art; while this aim itself will be disclosed to the common understanding, past all mistaking, by the actual bodily man with all his warmth of life. Of all artistic things, the most directly understandable is the Dramatic-Action (*Handlung*), for reason that its art is not complete until every helping artifice be cast behind it, as it were, and genuine life attain the faithfullest and most intelligible show. And thus each branch of art can only address itself to the *understanding* in proportion as its core—whose relation to Man, or derivation from him, alone can animate and justify the artwork—is ripening toward the Drama. In proportion as it passes over into Drama, as it pulses with the Drama's light, will each domain of Art grow all-intelligible, completely understood and justified. (2)

On to the stage, prepared by architect and painter, now steps Artistic Man, as Natural Man steps on the stage of Nature. What the statuary and the historical painter endeavoured to limn on *stone* or *canvas*, they now limn upon *themselves*, their form, their body's limbs, the features of their visage, and raise it to the consciousness of full artistic life. The same sense that led the sculptor in his grasp and rendering of the human figure, now leads the Mime in the handling and demeanour of his actual body. The same eye which taught the historical painter, in drawing and in colour, in arrangement of his drapery and composition of his groups, to find the beautiful, the graceful and the characteristic, now orders the whole breadth of *actual human show*. Sculptor and painter once freed the Greek Tragedian from his cothurnus and his mask, upon and under which the real man could only move according to a certain religious convention. With justice, did this pair of plastic artists annihilate the last disfigurement of pure artistic man, and thus prefigure in their stone and canvas the tragic Actor of the Future. As they once descried him in his undistorted truth, they now shall let him pass into reality and bring his form, in a measure sketched by them, to bodily portrayal with all its wealth of movement.

Thus the illusion of plastic art will turn to truth in Drama: the plastic artist will reach out hands to the dancer, to the *mime*, will lose himself in them, and thus become himself both mime and dancer.—So far as lies within his power, he will have to impart the inner man his feeling and his will-ing, to the eye. The breadth and depth of scenic space belong to him for the plastic message of his stature and his motion, as a single unit or in union with his fellows. But where his power ends, where the fulness of his will and feeling impels him to the *uttering* of the inner man by means of *Speech*, there will the Word proclaim his plain and conscious purpose: he becomes a *Poet* and, to be poet, a *tone-artist* (*Tonkünstler*). But as dancer, tone-artist, and poet, he still is one and the same thing: nothing other than *executant, artistic Man, who, in the fullest measure of his faculties, imparts himself to the highest expression of receptive power.*

It is in him, the immediate executant, that the three sister-arts unite their forces in one collective operation, in which the highest faculty of each comes to its highest unfolding. By working in common, each one of them attains the power to be and do the very thing which, of her own and inmost essence, she longs to do and be. Hereby: that each, where her own power ends, can be absorbed within the other, whose power commences where her's ends,—she maintains her own purity and freedom, her independence as that which she is.

The *mimetic dancer* is stripped of his impotence, so soon as he can sing and speak; the creations of *Tone* win all-explaining meaning through the mime, as well as through the poet's word, and that exactly in degree as Tone itself is able to transcend into the motion of the mime and the word of the poet; while the *Poet* first becomes a Man through his translation to the flesh and blood of the *Performer*: for though he metes to each artistic factor the guiding purpose which binds them all into a common whole, yet this purpose is first changed from "will" to "can" *by the poet's Will descending to the actor's Can.*

Not one rich faculty of the separate arts will remain unused in the United Artwork of the Future; in it will each attain its first complete appraisement. Thus, especially, will the manifold developments of Tone, so peculiar to our instrumental music, unfold their utmost wealth within this Artwork; nay, Tone will incite the mimetic art of Dance to entirely new discoveries, and no less swell the breath of Poetry to unimagined fill. For Music, in her solitude, has fashioned for herself an organ which is capable of the highest reaches of expression. This organ is the *Orchestra.* The tone-speech of Beethoven, introduced into Drama by the orchestra, marks an entirely fresh departure for the dramatic artwork. While Architecture and, more especially, scenic Landscape-painting have power to set the executant dramatic Artist in the surroundings of physical Nature, and to dower him from the exhaustless stores of natural phenomena with an ample and significant background,—so in the Orchestra, that pulsing body of many-coloured harmony, the personating individual Man is given, for his support, a stanchless elemental spring, at once artistic, natural, and human.

The Orchestra is, so to speak, the loam of endless, universal Feeling, from which the individual feeling of the separate actor draws power to shoot aloft to fullest height of growth: it, in a sense, dissolves (3) the hard immobile ground of the actual scene into a fluent, elastic, impressionable æther, whose unmeasured bottom is the great sea of Feeling itself. Thus the Orchestra is like the *Earth* from which Antæus, so soon as ever his foot had grazed it, drew new immortal life-force.

By its essence diametrically opposed to the scenic landscape which surrounds the actor, and therefore, as to locality, most rightly placed in the deepened foreground outside the scenic frame, it at like time forms the perfect complement of these surroundings; inasmuch as it broadens out the exhaustless *physical* element of Nature to the equally exhaustless *emotional* element of artistic Man. These elements, thus knit together, enclose the performer as with an atmospheric ring of Art and Nature, in which, hike to the heavenly bodies, he moves secure in fullest orbit, and whence, withal, he is free to radiate on every side his feelings and his views of life,—broadened to infinity, and showered, as it were, on distances as measureless as those on which the stars of heaven cast their rays of light.

Thus supplementing one another in their changeful dance, the united sister-arts will show themselves and make good their claim; now all together, now in pairs, and again in solitary splendour, according to the momentary need of the only rule- and purpose-giver, the Dramatic Action. Now plastic Mimicry will listen to the passionate plaint of Thought; now resolute Thought will pour itself into the expressive mould of Gesture; now Tone must vent alone the stream of Feeling, the shudder of alarm; and now, in mutual embrace, all three will raise the Will of Drama to immediate and potent Deed. For One thing there is that all the three united arts must will, in order to be free: and that one thing is the Drama: the reaching of the Drama's aim must be their common goal. Are they conscious of this aim, do they put forth all their will to work out that alone: so will they also gain the power to lop off from their several stems the egoistic offshoots of their own peculiar being; that therewith the tree may not spread out in formless mass to every wind of heaven, but proudly lift its wreath of branches, boughs and leaves, into its lofty crown.

The nature of Man, like that of every branch of Art, is manifold and over-fruitful: but *one thing* alone is the Soul of every unit, its most imperious bent (*Nothwendigster Trieb*), its strongest need-urged impulse. When this One Thing is recognised by man as his fundamental essence, then, to reach this One and indispensable, he has power to ward off every weaker, subordinated appetite, each feeble wish, whose satisfaction might stand between him and Its attainment. Only the weak and impotent knows no imperious, no mightiest longing of the soul: for him each instant is ruled by accidental, externally incited appetites which, for reason that they are but appetites, he never can allay; and therefore, hurled capriciously from one upon another, to and fro, he never can attain a real enjoyment. But should this need-reft one have strength to obstinately follow the appeasement of his accidental appetite, there then crop up in Life and Art those hideous, unnatural apparitions, the parasites of headlong egoistic frenzy, which fill us with such untold loathing in the murderous lust of despots, or in the wantonness of—modern operatic music. If the individual, however, feel in himself a mighty longing, an impulse that forces back all other desires, and forms the necessary inner urgence which constitutes his soul and being; and if he put forth all his force to satisfy it: he thus will also lift aloft his own peculiar force, and all his special faculties, to the fullest strength and height that e'er can lie within his reach.

But the individual man, in full possession of health of body, heart, and mind, can experience no higher need than that which is common to all his kind; for, to be a *true* Need, it can only be such an one as he can satisfy in Community alone. The most imperious and strongest need of full-fledged artist-man, however, is to impart himself in highest compass of his being to the fullest expression of Community; and .this he only reaches with the necessary breadth of general understanding in the *Drama*. In Drama he broadens out his own particular being, by the portrayal of an individual personality not his own, to a universally human being. He must completely step outside himself, to grasp the inner nature of an alien personality with that completeness which is needful before he can portray it. This he will only Attain when he so exhaustively analyses this individual in his contact with and penetration and completion by other individualities,—and therefore also the nature of these other individualities themselves,—when he forms thereof so lively a conception, that he gains a sympathetic feeling of this complementary influence on his own interior being. The perfectly artistic Performer is, therefore, the unit Man expanded to the *essence* of the *Human Species* by the utmost evolution of his own particular nature.

The place in which this wondrous process comes to pass, is the *Theatric* stage; the collective art-work which it brings to light of day, the *Drama*. But to force his own specific nature to the highest blossoming of its contents in this one and highest art-work, the separate artist, like each several art, must quell each selfish, arbitrary bent toward untimely bushing into outgrowths unfurthersome to the whole; the better then to put forth all his strength for reaching of the highest common purpose, which cannot indeed be realised without the unit, nor, on the other hand, without the unit's recurrent limitation.

This purpose of the Drama, is withal the only true artistic purpose that ever can be fully *realised*; whatsoever lies aloof from that, must necessarily lose itself in the sea of things indefinite, obscure, unfree. This purpose, however, the separate art-branch will never reach *alone*, (4) but only *all together*; and therefore the most *universal* is at like time the only real, free, the only universally *intelligible* Art-work.

-(1849)

Notes

(1) The problem of the Theatrical edifice of the Future can in no wise be considered as solved by our modern stage buildings: for they are laid out in accord with traditional laws and canons which have nothing in common with the requirements of pure Art. Where speculation for gain, on the one side, joins forces with luxurious ostentation on the other, the absolute interests of Art must be cryingly affected; and thus no architect in the world will be able to raise our stratified and fenced-off auditoria—dictated by the parcelling of our public into the most diverse categories of class and civil station—to conformity with any law of beauty. If one imagine oneself, for a moment, within the walls of the common Theatre of the Future, one will recognise with little trouble, that an undreamt width of field lies therein open for invention.— R. WAGNER.

(2) It can scarcely be indifferent to the modern landscape-painter to observe by how few his work is really understood to-day, and with what blear-eyed stupidity his nature-paintings are devoured by the Philistine world that pays for them; how the so-called "charming prospect" is purchased to assuage the idle, unintelligent, visual gluttony of those same need-less men whose sense of hearing is tickled by our modern, empty music-manufacture to that idiotic joy which is as repugnant a reward of his performance to the artist as it fully answers the intention of the artisan. Between the "charming prospect" and the "pretty tune" of our modern times there subsists a doleful affinity, whose bond of union is certainly not the musing calm of Thought, but that vulgar slipshod sentimentality which draws back in selfish horror from the sight of human suffering in its surroundings, to hire for itself a private heavenlet in the blue mists of Nature's generality. These sentimentals are willing enough to see and hear everything: only *not the actual, undistorted Man, who lifts his warning finger on the threshold of their dreams. But this is the very man whom we must set up in the forefront of our show!*—R. WAGNER.

(3) It is a little difficult to quite unravel this part of the metaphor, for the same word "Boden" is used twice over. I have thought it best to translate it in the first place as "loam," and in the second as "ground"; for it appears as though the idea were, in the former case, that of what agriculturists call a "top-dressing," and thus a substance which could break up the lower soil and make it fruitful. The "it" which occurs after the colon may refer either to the "feeling" or to the "orchestra," for both are neuter nouns.—TR.

(4) The modern *Playwright* will feel little tempted to concede that Drama ought not to belong exclusively to *his* branch of art, the art of *Poesy*; above all will he not be able to constrain himself to share it with the Tone-poet,—to wit, as he understands us, allow the Play to be swallowed up by the Opera. Perfectly correct!—so long as Opera subsists, the Play must also stand, and, for the matter of that, the Pantomime too; so long as any dispute hereon is thinkable, the Drama of the Future must itself remain un-thinkable. If, however, the Poet's doubt lie deeper, and consist in this, that he cannot conceive how Song should be entitled to usurp entirely the place of spoken dialogue: then he must take for rejoinder, that in two several regards he has not as yet a clear idea of the character of the Art-work of the Future. Firstly, he does not reflect that Music has to occupy a very different position in this Art-work to what she takes in modern Opera: that only where her power is the *fittest*, has she to open out her full expanse; while, on the contrary, wherever another power, for instance that of dramatic Speech, is the most *necessary*, she has to subordinate herself to that; still, that Music possesses the peculiar faculty of, without entirely keeping silence, so imperceptibly linking herself to the thought-full element of Speech that she lets the latter seem to walk abroad alone, the while she still supports it. Should the poet acknowledge this, then he has to recognise in the second place, that thoughts and situations to which the lightest and most restrained accompaniment of Music should seem importunate and burdensome, can only be such as are borrowed from the spirit of our modern Play; which, from beginning to end, will find no inch of breathing-space within the Art-work of the Future. The Man who will portray himself in the Drama of the Future has done for ever with all the prosaic hurly-burly of fashionable manners or polite intrigue, which our modern "poets"

have to tangle and to disentangle in their plays, with greatest circumstantiality. His nature-bidden action and his speech are: Yea, yea! and Nay, nay !—and all beyond is evil, i.e. modern and superfluous.—R. WAGNER.

The Work of Art in the Age of Mechanical Reproduction
by Walter Benjamin

"Our fine arts were developed, their types and uses were established, in times very different from the present, by men whose power of action upon things was insignificant in comparison with ours. But the amazing growth of our techniques, the adaptability and precision they have attained, the ideas and habits they are creating, make it a certainty that profound changes are impending in the ancient craft of the Beautiful. In all the arts there is a physical component which can no longer be considered or treated as it used to be, which cannot remain unaffected by our modern knowledge and power. For the last twenty years neither matter nor space nor time has been what it was from time immemorial. We must expect great innovations to transform the entire technique of the arts, thereby affecting artistic invention itself and perhaps even bringing about an amazing change in our very notion of art."

(Paul Valéry, Pièces sur L'Art, "Le Conquète de l'ubiquité", Paris. Quoted from Paul Valéry, *Aesthetics,* "The Conquest of Ubiquity", translated by Ralph Manheim, p. 225, Pantheon Books, Bollingen Series, New York, 1964.)

Preface

When Marx undertook his critique of the capitalistic mode of production, this mode was in its infancy. Marx directed his efforts in such a way as to give them prognostic value. He went back to the basic conditions underlying capitalistic production and through his presentation showed what could be expected of capitalism in the future. The result was that one could expect it not only to exploit the proletariat with increasing intensity, but ultimately to create conditions which would make it possible to abolish capitalism itself.

The transformation of the superstructure, which takes place far more slowly than that of the substructure, has taken more than half a century to manifest in all areas of culture the change in the conditions of production. Only today can it be indicated what form this has taken. Certain prognostic requirements should be met by these statements. However, theses about the art of the proletariat after its assumption of power or about the art of a classless society would have less bearing on these demands than theses about the developmental tendencies of art under present conditions of production. Their dialectic is no less noticeable in the superstructure than in the economy. It would therefore be wrong to underestimate the value of such theses as a weapon. They brush aside a number of outmoded concepts, such as creativity and genius, eternal value and mystery – concepts whose uncontrolled (and at present almost uncontrollable) application would lead to a processing of data in the Fascist sense. The concepts which are introduced into the theory of art in what follows differ from the more familiar terms in that they are completely useless for the purposes of Fascism. They are, on the other hand, useful for the formulation of revolutionary demands in the politics of art.

I

In principle a work of art has always been reproducible. Man-made artifacts could always be imitated by men. Replicas were made by pupils in practice of their craft, by masters for diffusing their works, and, finally, by third parties in the pursuit of gain. Mechanical reproduction of a work of art, however, represents something new. Historically, it advanced intermittently and in leaps at long intervals, but with accelerated intensity. The Greeks knew only two procedures of technically reproducing works of art: founding and stamping. Bronzes, terra cottas, and coins were the only art works which they could produce in quantity. All others were unique and could not be mechanically reproduced. With the woodcut graphic art became mechanically reproducible for the first time, long before script became reproducible by print. The enormous changes which printing, the mechanical reproduction of writing, has brought about in literature are a familiar story. However, within the phenomenon which we are here examining from the perspective of world history, print is merely a special, though particularly important, case. During the Middle Ages engraving and etching were added to the woodcut; at the beginning of the nineteenth century lithography made its appearance.

With lithography the technique of reproduction reached an essentially new stage. This much more direct process was distinguished by the tracing of the design on a stone rather than its incision on a block of wood or its etching on a copperplate and permitted graphic art for the first time to put its products on the market, not only in large numbers as hitherto, but also in daily changing forms. Lithography enabled graphic art to illustrate everyday life, and it began to keep pace with printing. But only a few decades after its invention, lithography was surpassed by photography. For the first time in the process of pictorial reproduction, photography freed the hand of the most important artistic functions which henceforth devolved only upon the eye looking into a lens. Since the eye perceives more swiftly than the hand can draw, the process of pictorial reproduction was accelerated so enormously that it could keep pace with speech. A film operator shooting a scene in the studio captures the images at the speed of an actor's speech. Just as lithography virtually implied the illustrated newspaper, so did photography foreshadow the sound film. The technical reproduction of sound was tackled at the end of the last century. These convergent endeavors made predictable a situation which Paul Valery pointed up in this sentence: "Just as water, gas, and electricity are brought into our houses from far off to satisfy our needs in response to a minimal effort, so we shall be supplied with visual or auditory images, which will appear and disappear at a simple movement of the hand, hardly more than a sign" (*op. cit.,* p. 226). Around 1900 technical reproduction had reached a standard that not only permitted it to reproduce all transmitted works of art and thus to cause the most profound change in their impact upon the public; it also had captured a place of its own among the artistic processes. For the study of this standard nothing is more revealing than the nature of the repercussions that these two different manifestations – the reproduction of works of art and the art of the film – have had on art in its traditional form.

II

Even the most perfect reproduction of a work of art is lacking in one element: its presence in time and space, its unique existence at the place where it happens to be. This unique existence of the work of art determined the history to which it was subject throughout the time of its existence. This includes the changes which it may have suffered in physical condition over the years as well as the various changes in its ownership. (1) The traces of the first can be revealed only by chemical or physical analyses which it is impossible to perform on a reproduction; changes of ownership are subject to a tradition which must be traced from the situation of the original.

The presence of the original is the prerequisite to the concept of authenticity. Chemical analyses of the patina of a bronze can help to establish this, as does the proof that a given manuscript of the Middle Ages stems from an archive of the fifteenth century. The whole sphere of authenticity is outside technical – and, of course, not only technical – reproducibility. (2) Confronted with its manual reproduction, which was usually branded as a forgery, the original preserved all its authority; not so *vis à vis* technical reproduction. The reason is twofold. First, process reproduction is more independent of the original than manual reproduction. For example, in photography, process reproduction can bring out those aspects of the original that are unattainable to the naked eye yet accessible to the lens, which is adjustable and chooses its angle at will. And photographic reproduction, with the aid of certain processes, such as enlargement or slow motion, can capture images which escape natural vision. Secondly, technical reproduction can put the copy of the original into situations which would be out of reach for the original itself. Above all, it enables the original to meet the beholder halfway, be it in the form of a photograph or a phonograph record. The cathedral leaves its locale to be received in the studio of a lover of art; the choral production, performed in an auditorium or in the open air, resounds in the drawing room.

The situations into which the product of mechanical reproduction can be brought may not touch the actual work of art, yet the quality of its presence is always depreciated. This holds not only for the art work but also, for instance, for a landscape which passes in review before the spectator in a movie. In the case of the art object, a most sensitive nucleus – namely, its authenticity – is interfered with whereas no natural object is vulnerable on that score. The authenticity of a thing is the essence of all that is transmissible from its beginning, ranging from its substantive duration to its testimony to the history which it has experienced. Since the historical testimony rests on the authenticity, the former, too, is jeopardized by reproduction when substantive duration ceases to matter. And what is really jeopardized when the historical testimony is affected is the authority of the object. (3)

One might subsume the eliminated element in the term "aura" and go on to say: that which withers in the age of mechanical reproduction is the aura of the work of art. This is a symptomatic process whose significance points beyond the realm of art. One might generalize by saying: the technique of reproduction detaches the reproduced object from the domain of tradition. By making many reproductions it substitutes a plurality of copies for a unique existence. And in permitting the reproduction to meet the beholder or listener in his own particular situation, it reactivates the object reproduced. These two processes lead to a tremendous shattering of tradition which is the obverse of the contemporary crisis and renewal of mankind. Both processes are intimately connected with the contemporary mass movements. Their most powerful agent is the film. Its social significance, particularly in its most positive form, is inconceivable without its destructive, cathartic aspect, that is, the liquidation of the traditional value of the cultural heritage. This phenomenon is most palpable in the great historical films. It extends to ever new positions. In 1927 Abel Gance exclaimed enthusiastically: "Shakespeare, Rembrandt, Beethoven will make films... all legends, all mythologies and all myths, all founders of religion, and the very religions... await their exposed resurrection, and the heroes crowd each other at the gate." (Abel Gance, "Le Temps de l'image est venu", *L'Art cinématographique,* Vol. 2, pp. 94 f, Paris 1927.) Presumably without intending it, he issued an invitation to a far-reaching liquidation.

III

During long periods of history, the mode of human sense perception changes with humanity's entire mode of existence. The manner in which human sense perception is organized, the medium in which it is accomplished, is determined not only by nature but by historical circumstances as well. The fifth century, with its great shifts of population, saw the birth of the late Roman art industry and the Vienna Genesis, and there developed not only an art different from that of antiquity but also a new kind of perception. The scholars of the Viennese school, Riegl and Wickhoff, who resisted the weight of classical tradition under which these later art forms had been buried, were the first to draw conclusions from them concerning the organization of perception at the time. However far-reaching their insight, these scholars limited themselves to showing the significant, formal hallmark which characterized perception in late Roman times. They did not attempt – and, perhaps, saw no way – to show the social transformations expressed by these changes of perception. The conditions for an analogous insight are more favorable in the present. And if changes in the medium of contemporary perception can be comprehended as decay of the aura, it is possible to show its social causes.

The concept of aura which was proposed above with reference to historical objects may usefully be illustrated with reference to the aura of natural ones. We define the aura of the latter as the unique phenomenon of a distance, however close it may be. If, while resting on a summer afternoon, you follow with your eyes a mountain range on the horizon or a branch which casts its shadow over you, you experience the aura of those mountains, of that branch. This image makes it easy to comprehend the social bases of the contemporary decay of the aura. It rests on two circumstances, both of which are related to the increasing significance of the masses in contemporary life. Namely, the desire of contemporary masses to bring things "closer" spatially and humanly, which is just as ardent as their bent toward overcoming the uniqueness of every reality by accepting its reproduction. (4) Every day the urge grows stronger to get hold of an object at very close range by way of its likeness, its reproduction. Unmistakably, reproduction as offered by picture magazines and newsreels differs from the image seen by the unarmed eye. Uniqueness and permanence are as closely linked in the latter as are transitoriness and reproducibility in the former. To pry an object from its shell, to destroy its aura, is the mark of a perception whose "sense of the universal equality of things" has increased to such a degree that it extracts it even from a unique object by means of reproduction. Thus is manifested in the field of perception what in the theoretical sphere is noticeable in the increasing importance of statistics. The adjustment of reality to the masses and of the masses to reality is a process of unlimited scope, as much for thinking as for perception.

IV

The uniqueness of a work of art is inseparable from its being imbedded in the fabric of tradition. This tradition itself is thoroughly alive and extremely changeable. An ancient statue of Venus, for example, stood in a different traditional context with the Greeks, who made it an object of veneration, than with the clerics of the Middle Ages, who viewed it as an ominous idol. Both of them, however, were equally confronted with its uniqueness, that is, its aura. Originally the contextual integration of art in tradition found its expression in the cult. We know that the earliest art works originated in the service of a ritual – first the magical, then the religious kind. It is significant that the existence of the work of art with reference to its aura is never entirely separated from its ritual function. In other words, the unique value of the "authentic" work of art has its basis in ritual, the location of its original use value. This ritualistic basis, however remote, is still recognizable as secularized ritual even in the most profane forms of the cult of beauty. (6) The secular cult of beauty, developed during the Renaissance and prevailing for three centuries, clearly showed that ritualistic basis in its decline and the first deep crisis which befell it. With the advent of the first truly revolutionary means of reproduction, photography, simultaneously with the rise of socialism, art sensed the approaching crisis which has become evident a century later. At the time, art reacted with the doctrine of *l'art pour l'art*, that is, with a theology of art. This gave rise to what might be called a negative theology in the form of the idea of "pure" art, which not only denied any social function of art but also any categorizing by subject matter. (In poetry, Mallarme was the first to take this position.)

An analysis of art in the age of mechanical reproduction must do justice to these relationships, for they lead us to an all-important insight: for the first time in world history, mechanical reproduction emancipates the work of art from its parasitical dependence on ritual. To an ever greater degree the work of art reproduced becomes the work of art designed for reproducibility. (7) From a photographic negative, for example, one can make any number of prints; to ask for the "authentic" print makes no sense. But the instant the criterion of authenticity ceases to be applicable to artistic production, the total function of art is reversed. Instead of being based on ritual, it begins to be based on another practice – politics.

V

Works of art are received and valued on different planes. Two polar types stand out; with one, the accent is on the cult value; with the other, on the exhibition value of the work. (8) Artistic production begins with ceremonial objects destined to serve in a cult. One may assume that what mattered was their existence, not their being on view. The elk portrayed by the man of the Stone Age on the walls of his cave was an instrument of magic. He did expose it to his fellow men, but in the main it was meant for the spirits. Today the cult value would seem to demand that the work of art remain hidden. Certain statues of gods are accessible only to the priest in the cella; certain Madonnas remain covered nearly all year round; certain sculptures on medieval cathedrals are invisible to the spectator on ground level. With the emancipation of the various art practices from ritual go increasing opportunities for the exhibition of their products. It is easier to exhibit a portrait bust that can be sent here and there than to exhibit the statue of a divinity that has its fixed place in the interior of a temple. The same holds for the painting as against the mosaic or fresco that preceded it. And even though the public presentability of a mass originally may have been just as great as that of a symphony, the latter originated at the moment when its public presentability promised to surpass that of the mass.

With the different methods of technical reproduction of a work of art, its fitness for exhibition increased to such an extent that the quantitative shift between its two poles turned into a qualitative transformation of its nature. This is comparable to the situation of the work of art in prehistoric times when, by the absolute emphasis on its cult value, it was, first and foremost, an instrument of magic. Only later did it come to be recognized as a work of art. In the same way today, by the absolute emphasis on its exhibition value the work of art becomes a creation with entirely new functions, among which the one we are conscious of, the artistic function, later may be recognized as incidental. (9) This much is certain: today photography and the film are the most serviceable exemplifications of this new function.

VI

In photography, exhibition value begins to displace cult value all along the line. But cult value does not give way without resistance. It retires into an ultimate retrenchment: the human countenance. It is no accident that the portrait was the focal point of early photography. The cult of remembrance of loved ones, absent or dead, offers a last refuge for the cult value of the picture. For the last time the aura emanates from the early photographs in the fleeting expression of a human face. This is what constitutes their melancholy, incomparable beauty. But as man withdraws from the photographic image, the exhibition value for the first time shows its superiority to the ritual value. To have pinpointed this new stage constitutes the incomparable significance of Atget, who, around 1900, took photographs of deserted Paris streets. It has quite justly been said of him that he photographed them like scenes of crime. The scene of a crime, too, is deserted; it is photographed for the purpose of establishing evidence. With Atget, photographs become standard evidence for historical occurrences, and acquire a hidden political significance. They demand a specific kind of approach; free-floating contemplation is not appropriate to them. They stir the viewer; he feels challenged by them in a new way. At the same time picture magazines begin to put up signposts for him, right ones or wrong ones, no matter. For the first time, captions have become obligatory. And it is clear that they have an altogether different character than the title of a painting. The directives which the captions give to those looking at pictures in illustrated magazines soon become even more explicit and more imperative in the film where the meaning of each single picture appears to be prescribed by the sequence of all preceding ones.

VII

The nineteenth-century dispute as to the artistic value of painting versus photography today seems devious and confused. This does not diminish its importance, however; if anything, it underlines it. The dispute was in fact the symptom of a historical transformation the universal impact of which was not realized by either of the rivals. When the age of mechanical reproduction separated art from its basis in cult, the semblance of its autonomy disappeared forever. The resulting change in the function of art transcended the perspective of the century; for a long time it even escaped that of the twentieth century, which experienced the development of the film.

Earlier much futile thought had been devoted to the question of whether photography is an art. The primary question – whether the very invention of photography had not transformed the entire nature of art – was not raised. Soon the film theoreticians asked the same ill-considered question with regard to the film. But the difficulties which photography caused traditional aesthetics were mere child's play as compared to those raised by the film. Whence the insensitive and forced character of early theories of the film. Abel Gance, for instance, compares the film with hieroglyphs: "Here, by a remarkable regression, we have come back to the level of expression of the

Egyptians ... Pictorial language has not yet matured because our eyes have not yet adjusted to it. There is as yet insufficient respect for, insufficient cult of, what it expresses." (Abel Gance, *op. cit.,* pp. 100-1) Or, in the words of Séverin-Mars: "What art has been granted a dream more poetical and more real at the same time! Approached in this fashion the film might represent an incomparable means of expression. Only the most high-minded persons, in the most perfect and mysterious moments of their lives, should be allowed to enter its ambience." (Séverin-Mars, quoted by Abel Gance, *op. cit.,* p. 100) Alexandre Arnoux concludes his fantasy about the silent film with the question: "Do not all the bold descriptions we have given amount to the definition of prayer?" (Alexandre Arnoux, *Cinéma pris,* 1929, p. 28) It is instructive to note how their desire to class the film among the "arts" forces these theoreticians to read ritual elements into it – with a striking lack of discretion. Yet when these speculations were published, films like *L'Opinion publique* and *The Gold Rush* had already appeared. This, however, did not keep Abel Gance from adducing hieroglyphs for purposes of comparison, nor Séverin-Mars from speaking of the film as one might speak of paintings by Fra Angelico. Characteristically, even today ultrareactionary authors give the film a similar contextual significance – if not an outright sacred one, then at least a supernatural one. Commenting on Max Reinhardt's film version of *A Midsummer Night's Dream*, Werfel states that undoubtedly it was the sterile copying of the exterior world with its streets, interiors, railroad stations, restaurants, motorcars, and beaches which until now had obstructed the elevation of the film to the realm of art. "The film has not yet realized its true meaning, its real possibilities ... these consist in its unique faculty to express by natural means and with incomparable persuasiveness all that is fairylike, marvelous, supernatural." (Franz Werfel, „Ein Sommernachtstraum, Ein Film von Shakespeare und Reinhardt", *Neues Wiener Journal,* cited in *Lu,* November, 1935)

VIII

The artistic performance of a stage actor is definitely presented to the public by the actor in person; that of the screen actor, however, is presented by a camera, with a twofold consequence. The camera that presents the performance of the film actor to the public need not respect the performance as an integral whole. Guided by the cameraman, the camera continually changes its position with respect to the performance. The sequence of positional views which the editor composes from the material supplied him constitutes the completed film. It comprises certain factors of movement which are in reality those of the camera, not to mention special camera angles, close-ups, etc. Hence, the performance of the actor is subjected to a series of optical tests. This is the first consequence of the fact that the actor's performance is presented by means of a camera. Also, the film actor lacks the opportunity of the stage actor to adjust to the audience during his performance, since he does not present his performance to the audience in person. This permits the audience to take the position of a critic, without experiencing any personal contact with the actor. The audience's identification with the actor is really an identification with the camera. Consequently the audience takes the position of the camera; its approach is that of testing. (10) This is not the approach to which cult values may be exposed.

IX

For the film, what matters primarily is that the actor represents himself to the public before the camera, rather than representing someone else. One of the first to sense the actor's metamorphosis by this form of testing was Pirandello. Though his remarks on the subject in his novel *Si Gira* were limited to the negative aspects of the question and to the silent film only, this hardly impairs their validity. For in this respect, the sound film did not change anything essential. What matters is that the part is acted not for an audience but for a mechanical contrivance – in the case of the sound film, for two of them. "The film actor," wrote Pirandello, "feels as if in exile – exiled not only from the stage but also from himself. With a vague sense of discomfort he feels inexplicable emptiness: his body loses its corporeality, it evaporates, it is deprived of reality, life, voice, and the noises caused by his moving about, in order to be changed into a mute image, flickering an instant on the screen, then vanishing into silence .... The projector will play with his shadow before the public, and he himself must be content to play before the camera." (Luigi Pirandello, *Si Gira,* quoted by Léon Pierre-Quint, "Signification du cinéma", *L'art cinématographique, op. cit.,* pp. 14-15) This situation might also be characterized as follows: for the first time – and this is the effect of the film – man has to operate with his whole living person, yet forgoing its aura. For aura is tied to his presence; there can be no replica of it. The aura which, on the stage, emanates from Macbeth, cannot be separated for the spectators from that of the actor. However, the singularity of the shot in the studio is that the camera is substituted for the public. Consequently, the aura that envelops the actor vanishes, and with it the aura of the figure he portrays.

It is not surprising that it should be a dramatist such as Pirandello who, in characterizing the film, inadvertently touches on the very crisis in which we see the theater. Any thorough study proves that there is indeed no greater contrast than that of the stage play to a work of art that is completely subject to or, like the film, founded in, mechanical reproduction. Experts have long recognized that in the film "the greatest effects are almost always obtained by 'acting' as little as possible ... " In 1932 Rudolf Arnheim saw "the latest trend ... in treating the actor as a stage prop chosen for its characteristics and... inserted at the proper place." (11) With this idea something else is closely connected. The stage actor identifies himself with the character of his role. The film actor very often is denied this opportunity. His creation is by no means all of a piece; it is composed of many separate performances. Besides certain fortuitous considerations, such as cost of studio, availability of fellow players, décor, etc., there are elementary necessities of equipment that split the actor's work into a series of mountable episodes. In particular, lighting and its installation require the presentation of an event that, on the screen, unfolds as a rapid and unified scene, in a sequence of separate shootings which may take hours at the studio; not to mention more obvious montage. Thus a jump from the window can be shot in the studio as a jump from a scaffold, and the ensuing flight, if need be, can be shot weeks later when outdoor scenes are taken. Far more paradoxical cases can easily be construed. Let us assume that an actor is supposed to be startled by a knock at the door. If his reaction is not satisfactory, the director can resort to an expedient: when the actor happens to be at the studio again he has a shot fired behind him without his being forewarned of it. The frightened reaction can be shot now and be cut into the screen version. Nothing more strikingly shows that art has left the realm of the "beautiful semblance" which, so far, had been taken to be the only sphere where art could thrive.

X

The feeling of strangeness that overcomes the actor before the camera, as Pirandello describes it, is basically of the same kind as the estrangement felt before one's own image in the mirror. But now the reflected image has become separable, transportable. And where is it transported? Before the public. (12) Never for a moment does the screen actor cease to be conscious of this fact. While facing the camera he knows that ultimately he will face the public, the consumers who constitute the market. This market, where he offers not only his labor but also his whole self, his heart and soul, is beyond his reach. During the shooting he has as little contact with it as any article made in a factory. This may contribute to that oppression, that new anxiety which, according to Pirandello, grips the actor before the camera. The film responds to the shriveling of the aura with an artificial build-up of the "personality" outside the studio. The cult of the movie star, fostered by the money of the film industry, preserves not the unique aura of the person but the "spell of the personality," the phony spell of a commodity. So long as the movie-makers' capital sets the fashion, as a rule no other revolutionary merit can be accredited to today's film than the promotion of a revolutionary criticism of traditional concepts of art. We do not deny that in some cases today's films can also promote revolutionary criticism of social conditions, even of the distribution of property. However, our present study is no more specifically concerned with this than is the film production of Western Europe.

It is inherent in the technique of the film as well as that of sports that everybody who witnesses its accomplishments is somewhat of an expert. This is obvious to anyone listening to a group of newspaper boys leaning on their bicycles and discussing the outcome of a bicycle race. It is not for nothing that newspaper publishers arrange races for their delivery boys. These arouse great interest among the participants, for the victor has an opportunity to rise from delivery boy to professional racer. Similarly, the newsreel offers everyone the opportunity to rise from passer-by to movie extra. In this way any man might even find himself part of a work of art, as witness Vertov's *Three Songs About Lenin* or Ivens' *Borinage*. Any man today can lay claim to being filmed. This claim can best be elucidated by a comparative look at the historical situation of contemporary literature.

For centuries a small number of writers were confronted by many thousands of readers. This changed toward the end of the last century. With the increasing extension of the press, which kept placing new political, religious, scientific, professional, and local organs before the readers, an increasing number of readers became writers – at first, occasional ones. It began with the daily press opening to its readers space for "letters to the editor." And today there is hardly a gainfully employed European who could not, in principle, find an opportunity to publish somewhere or other comments on his work, grievances, documentary reports, or that sort of thing. Thus, the distinction between author and public is about to lose its basic character. The difference becomes merely functional; it may vary from case to case. At any moment the reader is ready to turn into a writer. As expert, which he had to become willy-nilly in an extremely specialized work process, even if only in some minor respect, the reader gains access to authorship. In the Soviet Union work itself is given a voice. To present it verbally is part of a man's ability to perform the work. Literary license is now founded on polytechnic rather than specialized training and thus becomes common property. (13)

All this can easily be applied to the film, where transitions that in literature took centuries have come about in a decade. In cinematic practice, particularly in Russia, this change-over has partially become established reality. Some of the players whom we meet in Russian films are not actors in our sense but people who portray themselves and primarily in their own work process. In Western Europe the capitalistic exploitation of the film denies consideration to modern man's legitimate claim to being reproduced. Under these circumstances the film industry is trying hard to spur the interest of the masses through illusion-promoting spectacles and dubious speculations.

XI

The shooting of a film, especially of a sound film, affords a spectacle unimaginable anywhere at any time before this. It presents a process in which it is impossible to assign to a spectator a viewpoint which would exclude from the actual scene such extraneous accessories as camera equipment, lighting machinery, staff assistants, etc. – unless his eye were on a line parallel with the lens. This circumstance, more than any other, renders superficial and insignificant any possible similarity between a scene in the studio and one on the stage. In the theater one is well aware of the place from which the play cannot immediately be detected as illusionary. There is no such place for the movie scene that is being shot. Its illusionary nature is that of the second degree, the result of cutting. That is to say, in the studio the mechanical equipment has penetrated so deeply into reality that its pure aspect freed from the foreign substance of equipment is the result of a special procedure, namely, the shooting by the specially adjusted camera and the mounting of the shot together with other similar ones. The equipment-free aspect of reality here has become the height of artifice; the sight of immediate reality has become an orchid in the land of technology.

Even more revealing is the comparison of these circumstances, which differ so much from those of the theater, with the situation in painting. Here the question is: How does the cameraman compare with the painter? To answer this we take recourse to an analogy with a surgical operation. The surgeon represents the polar opposite of the magician. The magician heals a sick person by the laying on of hands; the surgeon cuts into the patient's body. The magician maintains the natural distance between the patient and himself; though he reduces it very slightly by the laying on of hands, he greatly increases it by virtue of his authority. The surgeon does exactly the reverse; he greatly diminishes the distance between himself and the patient by penetrating into the patient's body, and increases it but little by the caution with which his hand moves among the organs. In short, in contrast to the magician - who is still hidden in the medical practitioner – the surgeon at the decisive moment abstains from facing the patient man to man; rather, it is through the operation that he penetrates into him.

Magician and surgeon compare to painter and cameraman. The painter maintains in his work a natural distance from reality, the cameraman penetrates deeply into its web. (14) There is a tremendous difference between the pictures they obtain. That of the painter is a total one, that of the cameraman consists of multiple fragments which are assembled under a new law. Thus, for contemporary man the representation of reality by the film is incomparably more significant than that of the painter, since it offers, precisely because of the thoroughgoing permeation of reality with mechanical equipment, an aspect of reality which is free of all equipment. And that is what one is entitled to ask from a work of art.

XII

Mechanical reproduction of art changes the reaction of the masses toward art. The reactionary attitude toward a Picasso painting changes into the progressive reaction toward a Chaplin movie. The progressive reaction is characterized by the direct, intimate fusion of visual and emotional enjoyment with the orientation of the expert. Such fusion is of great social significance. The greater the decrease in the social significance of an art form, the sharper the distinction between criticism and enjoyment by the public. The conventional is uncritically enjoyed, and the truly new is criticized with aversion. With regard to the screen, the critical and the receptive attitudes of the public coincide. The decisive reason for this is that individual reactions are predetermined by the mass audience response they are about to produce, and this is nowhere more pronounced than in the film. The moment these responses become manifest they control each other. Again, the comparison with painting is fruitful. A painting has always had an excellent chance to be viewed by one person or by a few. The simultaneous contemplation of paintings by a large public, such as developed in the nineteenth century, is an early symptom of the crisis of painting, a crisis which was by no means occasioned exclusively by photography but rather in a relatively independent manner by the appeal of art works to the masses.

Painting simply is in no position to present an object for simultaneous collective experience, as it was possible for architecture at all times, for the epic poem in the past, and for the movie today. Although this circumstance in itself should not lead one to conclusions about the social role of painting, it does constitute a serious threat as soon as painting, under special conditions and, as it were, against its nature, is confronted directly by the masses. In the churches and monasteries of the Middle Ages and at the princely courts up to the end of the eighteenth century, a collective reception of paintings did not occur simultaneously, but by graduated and hierarchized mediation. The change that has come about is an expression of the particular conflict in which painting was implicated by the mechanical reproducibility of paintings. Although paintings began to be publicly exhibited in galleries and salons, there was no way for the masses to organize and control themselves in their reception. (15) Thus the same public which responds in a progressive manner toward a grotesque film is bound to respond in a reactionary manner to surrealism.

XIII

The characteristics of the film lie not only in the manner in which man presents himself to mechanical equipment but also in the manner in which, by means of this apparatus, man can represent his environment. A glance at occupational psychology illustrates the testing capacity of the equipment. Psychoanalysis illustrates it in a different perspective. The film has enriched our field of perception with methods which can be illustrated by those of Freudian theory. Fifty years ago, a slip of the tongue passed more or less unnoticed. Only exceptionally may such a slip have revealed dimensions of depth in a conversation which had seemed to be taking its course on the surface. Since the *Psychopathology of Everyday Life* things have changed. This book isolated and made analyzable things which had heretofore floated along unnoticed in the broad stream of perception. For the entire spectrum of optical, and now also acoustical, perception the film has brought about a similar deepening of apperception. It is only an obverse of this fact that behavior items shown in a movie can be analyzed much more precisely and from more points of view than those presented on paintings or on the stage. As compared with painting, filmed behavior lends itself more readily to analysis because of its incomparably more precise statements of the situation. In comparison with the stage scene, the filmed behavior item lends itself more readily to analysis because it can be isolated more easily. This circumstance derives its chief importance from its tendency to promote the mutual penetration of art and science. Actually, of a screened behavior item which is neatly brought out in a certain situation, like a muscle of a body, it is difficult to say which is more fascinating, its artistic value or its value for science. To demonstrate the identity of the artistic and scientific uses of photography which heretofore usually were separated will be one of the revolutionary functions of the film. (16)

By close-ups of the things around us, by focusing on hidden details of familiar objects, by exploring common place milieus under the ingenious guidance of the camera, the film, on the one hand, extends our comprehension of the necessities which rule our lives; on the other hand, it manages to assure us of an immense and unexpected field of action. Our taverns and our metropolitan streets, our offices and furnished rooms, our railroad stations and our factories appeared to have us locked up hopelessly. Then came the film and burst this prison-world asunder by the dynamite of the tenth of a second, so that now, in the midst of its far-flung ruins and debris, we calmly and adventurously go traveling. With the close-up, space expands; with slow motion, movement is extended. The enlargement of a snapshot does not simply render more precise what in any case was visible, though unclear: it reveals entirely new structural formations of the subject. So, too, slow motion not only presents familiar qualities of movement but reveals in them entirely unknown ones "which, far from looking like retarded rapid movements, give the effect of singularly gliding, floating, supernatural motions." (Rudolf Arnheim, *loc. Cit.,* p. 138) Evidently a different nature opens itself to the camera than opens to the naked eye – if only because an unconsciously penetrated space is substituted for a space consciously explored by man. Even if one has a general knowledge of the way people walk, one knows nothing of a person's posture during the fractional second of a stride. The act of reaching for a lighter or a spoon is familiar routine, yet we hardly know what really goes on between hand and metal, not to mention how this fluctuates with our moods. Here the camera intervenes with the resources of its lowerings and liftings, its interruptions and isolations, it extensions and accelerations, its enlargements and reductions. The camera introduces us to unconscious optics as does psychoanalysis to unconscious impulses.

XIV

One of the foremost tasks of art has always been the creation of a demand which could be fully satisfied only later. (17) The history of every art form shows critical epochs in which a certain art form aspires to effects which could be fully obtained only with a changed technical standard, that is to say, in a new art form. The extravagances and crudities of art which thus appear, particularly in the so-called decadent epochs, actually arise from the nucleus of its richest historical energies. In recent years, such barbarisms were abundant in Dadaism. It is only now that its impulse becomes discernible: Dadaism attempted to create by pictorial – and literary – means the effects which the public today seeks in the film.

Every fundamentally new, pioneering creation of demands will carry beyond its goal. Dadaism did so to the extent that it sacrificed the market values which are so characteristic of the film in favor of higher ambitions – though of course it was not conscious of such intentions as here described. The Dadaists attached much less importance to the sales value of their work than to its usefulness for contemplative immersion. The studied degradation of their material was not the least of their means to achieve this uselessness. Their poems are "word salad" containing obscenities and every imaginable waste product of language. The same is true of their paintings, on which they mounted buttons and tickets. What they intended and achieved was a relentless destruction of the aura of their creations, which they branded as reproductions with the very means of production. Before a painting of Arp's or a poem by August Stramm it is impossible to take time for contemplation and evaluation as one would before a canvas of Derain's or a poem by Rilke. In the decline of middle-class society, contemplation became a school for asocial behavior; it was countered by distraction as a variant of social conduct. (18) Dadaistic activities actually assured a rather vehement distraction by making works of art the center of scandal. One requirement was foremost: to outrage the public.

From an alluring appearance or persuasive structure of sound the work of art of the Dadaists became an instrument of ballistics. It hit the spectator like a bullet, it happened to him, thus acquiring a tactile quality. It promoted a demand for the film, the distracting element of which is also primarily tactile, being based on changes of place and focus which periodically assail the spectator. Let us compare the screen on which a film unfolds with the canvas of a painting. The painting invites the spectator to contemplation; before it the spectator can abandon himself to his associations. Before the movie frame he cannot do so. No sooner has his eye grasped a scene than it is already changed. It cannot be arrested. Duhamel, who detests the film and knows nothing of its significance, though something of its structure, notes this circumstance as follows: "I can no longer think what I want to think. My thoughts have been replaced by moving images." (George Duhamel, *Scènes de la vie future,* Paris, 1930, p. 52) The spectator's process of association in view of these images is indeed interrupted by their constant, sudden change. This constitutes the shock effect of the film, which, like all shocks, should be cushioned by heightened presence of mind. By means of its technical structure, the film has taken the physical shock effect out of the wrappers in which Dadaism had, as it were, kept it inside the moral shock effect. (20)

XV

The mass is a matrix from which all traditional behavior toward works of art issues today in a new form. Quantity has been transmuted into quality. The greatly increased mass of participants has produced a change in the mode of participation. The fact that the new mode of participation first appeared in a disreputable form must not confuse the spectator. Yet some people have launched spirited attacks against precisely this superficial aspect. Among these, Duhamel has expressed himself in the most radical manner. What he objects to most is the kind of participation which the movie elicits from the masses. Duhamel calls the movie "a pastime for helots, a diversion for uneducated, wretched, worn-out creatures who are consumed by their worries a spectacle which requires no concentration and presupposes no intelligence which kindles no light in the heart and awakens no hope other than the ridiculous one of someday becoming a 'star' in Los Angeles." (Duhamel, *op. cit.*, p. 58) Clearly, this is at bottom the same ancient lament that the masses seek distraction whereas art demands concentration from the spectator. That is a commonplace. The question remains whether it provides a platform for the analysis of the film. A closer look is needed here. Distraction and concentration form polar opposites which may be stated as follows: A man who concentrates before a work of art is absorbed by it. He enters into this work of art the way legend tells of the Chinese painter when he viewed his finished painting. In contrast, the distracted mass absorbs the work of art. This is most obvious with regard to buildings. Architecture has always represented the prototype of a work of art the reception of which is consummated by a collectivity in a state of distraction. The laws of its reception are most instructive.

Buildings have been man's companions since primeval times. Many art forms have developed and perished. Tragedy begins with the Greeks, is extinguished with them, and after centuries its "rules" only are revived. The epic poem, which had its origin in the youth of nations, expires in Europe at the end of the Renaissance. Panel painting is a creation of the Middle Ages, and nothing guarantees its uninterrupted existence. But the human need for shelter is lasting. Architecture has never been idle. Its history is more ancient than that of any other art, and its claim to being a living force has significance in every attempt to comprehend the relationship of the masses to art. Buildings are appropriated in a twofold manner: by use and by perception – or rather, by touch and sight. Such appropriation cannot be understood in terms of the attentive concentration of a tourist before a famous building. On the tactile side there is no counterpart to contemplation on the optical side. Tactile appropriation is accomplished not so much by attention as by habit. As regards architecture, habit determines to a large extent even optical reception. The latter, too, occurs much less through rapt attention than by noticing the object in incidental fashion. This mode of appropriation, developed with reference to architecture, in certain circumstances acquires canonical value. For the tasks which face the human apparatus of perception at the turning points of history cannot be solved by optical means, that is, by contemplation, alone. They are mastered gradually by habit, under the guidance of tactile appropriation.

The distracted person, too, can form habits. More, the ability to master certain tasks in a state of distraction proves that their solution has become a matter of habit. Distraction as provided by art presents a covert control of the extent to which new tasks have become soluble by apperception. Since, moreover, individuals are tempted to avoid such tasks, art will tackle the most difficult and most important ones where it is able to mobilize the masses. Today it does so in the film. Reception in a state of distraction, which is increasing noticeably in all fields of art and is symptomatic of profound changes in apperception, finds in the film its true means of exercise. The film with its shock effect meets this mode of reception halfway. The film makes the cult value recede into the background not only by putting the public in the position of the critic, but also by the fact that at the movies this position requires no attention. The public is an examiner, but an absent-minded one.

Epilogue

The growing proletarianization of modern man and the increasing formation of masses are two aspects of the same process. Fascism attempts to organize the newly created proletarian masses without affecting the property structure which the masses strive to eliminate. Fascism sees its salvation in giving these masses not their right, but instead a chance to express themselves. (21) The masses have a right to change property relations; Fascism seeks to give them an expression while preserving property. The logical result of Fascism is the introduction of aesthetics into political life. The violation of the masses, whom Fascism, with its *Führer* cult, forces to their knees, has its counterpart in the violation of an apparatus which is pressed into the production of ritual values.

All efforts to render politics aesthetic culminate in one thing: war. War and war only can set a goal for mass movements on the largest scale while respecting the traditional property system. This is the political formula for the situation. The technological formula may be stated as follows: Only war makes it possible to mobilize all of today's technical resources while maintaining the property system. It goes without saying that the Fascist apotheosis of war does not employ such arguments. Still, Marinetti says in his manifesto on the Ethiopian colonial war:

"For twenty-seven years we Futurists have rebelled against the branding of war as anti-aesthetic ... Accordingly we state:... War is beautiful because it establishes man's dominion over the subjugated machinery by means of gas masks, terrifying megaphones, flame throwers, and small tanks. War is beautiful because it initiates the dreamt-of metalization of the human body. War is beautiful because it enriches a flowering meadow with the fiery orchids of machine guns. War is beautiful because it combines the gunfire, the cannonades, the cease-fire, the scents, and the stench of putrefaction into a symphony. War is beautiful because it creates new architecture, like that of the big tanks, the geometrical formation flights, the smoke spirals from burning villages, and many others ... Poets and artists of Futurism! ... remember these principles of an aesthetics of war so that your struggle for a new literature and a new graphic art ... may be illumined by them!"

This manifesto has the virtue of clarity. Its formulations deserve to be accepted by dialecticians. To the latter, the aesthetics of today's war appears as follows: If the natural utilization of productive forces is impeded by the property system, the increase in technical devices, in speed, and in the sources of energy will press for an unnatural utilization, and this is found in war. The destructiveness of war furnishes proof that society has not been mature enough to incorporate technology as its organ, that technology has not been sufficiently developed to cope with the elemental forces of society. The horrible features of imperialistic warfare are attributable to the discrepancy between the tremendous means of production and their inadequate utilization in the process of production – in other words, to unemployment and the lack of markets. Imperialistic war is a rebellion of technology which collects, in the form of "human material," the claims to which society has denied its natural materrial. Instead of draining rivers, society directs a human stream into a bed of trenches; instead of dropping seeds from airplanes, it drops incendiary bombs over cities; and through gas warfare the aura is abolished in a new way.

"Fiat ars – pereat mundus", says Fascism, and, as Marinetti admits, expects war to supply the artistic gratification of a sense perception that has been changed by technology. This is evidently the consummation of "l'art pour l'art." Mankind, which in Homer's time was an object of contemplation for the Olympian gods, now is one for itself. Its self-alienation has reached such a degree that it can experience its own destruction as an aesthetic pleasure of the first order. This is the situation of politics which Fascism is rendering aesthetic. Communism responds by politicizing art.

Notes

(1) Of course, the history of a work of art encompasses more than this. The history of the "Mona Lisa," for instance, encompasses the kind and number of its copies made in the 17th, 18th, and 19th centuries.

(2) Precisely because authenticity is not reproducible, the intensive penetration of certain (mechanical) processes of reproduction was instrumental in differentiating and grading authenticity. To develop such differentiations was an important function of the trade in works of art. The invention of the woodcut may be said to have struck at the root of the quality of authenticity even before its late flowering. To be sure, at the time of its origin a medieval picture of the Madonna could not yet be said to be "authentic." It became authentic only during the succeeding centuries and perhaps most strikingly so during the last one.

(3) The poorest provincial staging of *Faust* is superior to a Faust film in that, ideally, it competes with the first performance at Weimar. Before the screen it is unprofitable to remember traditional contents which might come to mind before the stage-for instance, that Goethe's friend Johann Heinrich Merck is hidden in Mephisto, and the like.

(4) To satisfy the human interest of the masses may mean to have ones social function removed from the field of vision. Nothing guarantees that a portraitist of today, when painting a famous surgeon at the breakfast table in the midst of his family, depicts his social function more precisely than a painter of the 17th century who portrayed his medical doctors as representing this profession, like Rembrandt in his "Anatomy Lesson."

(5) The definition of the aura as a "unique phenomenon of a distance however close it may be" represents nothing but the formulation of the cult value of the work of art in categories of space and time perception. Distance is the opposite of closeness. The essentially distant object is the unapproachable one. Unapproachability is indeed a major quality of the cult image. True to its

nature, it remains distant, however close it may be." The closeness which one may gain from its subject matter does not impair the distance which it retains in its appearance.

(6) To the extent to which the cult value of the painting is secularized the ideas of its fundamental uniqueness lose distinctness. In the imagination of the beholder the uniqueness of the phenomena which hold sway in the cult image is more and more displaced by the empirical uniqueness of the creator or of his creative achievement. To be sure, never completely so; the concept of authenticity always transcends mere genuineness. (This is particularly apparent in the collector who always retains some traces of the fetishist and who, by owning the work of art, shares in its ritual power.) Nevertheless, the function of the concept of authenticity remains determinate in the evaluation of art; with the secularization of art, authenticity displaces the cult value of the work.

(7) In the case of films, mechanical reproduction is not, as with literature and painting, an external condition for mass distribution. Mechanical reproduction is inherent in the very technique of film production. This technique not only permits in the most direct way but virtually causes mass distribution. It enforces distribution because the production of a film is so expensive that an individual who, for instance, might afford to buy a painting no longer can afford to buy a film. In 1927 it was calculated that a major film, in order to pay its way, had to reach an audience of nine million. With the sound film, to be sure, a setback in its international distribution occurred at first: audiences became limited by language barriers. This coincided with the Fascist emphasis on national interests. It is more important to focus on this connection with Fascism than on this set back, which was soon minimized by synchronization. The simultaneity of both phenomena is attributable to the depression. The same disturbances which, on a larger scale, led to an attempt to maintain the existing property structure by sheer force led the endangered film capital to speed up the development of the sound film. The introduction of the sound film brought about a temporary relief, not only because it again brought the masses into the theaters but also because it merged new capital

from the electrical industry with that of the film industry. Thus, viewed from the outside, the sound film promoted national interests, but seen from the inside it helped to internationalize film production even more than previously.

     (8) This polarity cannot come into its own in the aesthetics of Idealism. Its idea of beauty comprises these polar opposites without differentiating between them and consequently excludes their polarity. Yet in Hegel this polarity announces itself as clearly as possible within the limits of Idealism. We quote from his *Philosophy of History*:

     "Images were known of old. Piety at an early time required them for worship, but it could do without beautiful images. These might even be disturbing. In every beautiful painting there is also something nonspiritual, merely external, but its spirit speaks to man through its beauty. Worshipping, conversely, is concerned with the work as an object, for it is but a spiritless stupor of the soul. . . . Fine art has arisen ... in the church . . . , although it has already gone beyond its principle as art."

     Likewise, the following passage from *The Philosophy of Fine Art* indicates that Hegel sensed a problem here.

     "We are beyond the stage of reverence for works of art as divine and objects deserving our worship. The impression they produce is one of a more reflective kind, and the emotions they arouse require a higher test... "-G. W. F. Hegel, *The Philosophy of Fine Art*, trans., with notes, by F. P. B. Osmaston, Vol. I, p. 12, London, 1920.

     The transition from the first kind of artistic reception to the second characterizes the history of artistic reception in general. Apart from that, a certain oscillation between these two polar modes of reception can be demonstrated for each work of art Take the Sistine Madonna. Since Hubert Grimme's research it has been known that the Madonna originally was painted for the purpose of exhibition. Grimme's research was inspired by the question: What is the purpose of the molding in the foreground of the painting which the two cupids lean upon? How, Grimme asked further, did Raphael come to furnish the sky with two draperies? Research proved that the Madonna had been commissioned for the public lying-in-state of PopeSixtus. The Popes lay in State in a certain side chapel of St. Peter's. On that occasion Raphael's picture had been fastened in a nichelike background of the chapel, supported by the coffin. In this picture Raphael portrays the Madonna approaching the papal coffin in clouds from the background of the niche, which was demarcated by green drapes. At the obsequies of Sixtus a pre-eminent exhibition value of Raphael's picture was taken advantage of. Some time later it was placed on the high altar in the church of the Black Friars at Piacenza. The reason for this exile is to be found in the Roman rites which forbid the use of paintings exhibited at obsequies as cult objects on the high altar. This regulation devalued Raphael's picture to some degree. In order to obtain an adequate price nevertheless, the Papal See resolved to add to the bargain the tacit toleration of the picture above the high altar. To avoid attention the picture was given to the monks of the far-off provincial town.

(9) Bertolt Brecht, on a different level, engaged in analogous reflections: "If the concept of 'work of art' can no longer be applied to the thing that emerges once the work is transformed into a commodity, we have to eliminate this concept with cautious care but without fear, lest we liquidate the function of the very thing as well. For it has to go through this phase without mental reservation, and not as noncommittal deviation from the straight path; rather, what happens here with the work of art will change it fundamentally and erase its past to such an extent that should the old concept be taken up again-and it will, why not?-it will no longer stir any memory of the thing it once designated."

(10) "The film . . . provides-or could provide-useful insight into the details of human actions. . . . Character is never used as a source of motivation; the inner life of the persons never supplies the principal cause of the plot and seldom is its main result." (Bertolt Brecht, *Versuche*, "Der Dreigroschenprozess," p. 268.) The expansion of the field of the testable which mechanical equipment brings about for the actor corresponds to the extraordinary expansion of the field of the testable brought about for the individual through economic conditions. Thus, vocational aptitude tests become constantly more important. What matters in these tests are segmental performances of the individual. The film shot and the vocational aptitude test

are taken before a committee of experts. The camera director in the Studio occupies a place identical with that of the examiner during aptitude tests.

(11) Rudolf Arnheim, *Film als Kunst*, Berlin, 1932, pp. 176 f. In this context certain seemingly unimportant details in which the film director deviates from stage practices gain in interest. Such is the attempt to let the actor play without make-up, as made among others by Dreyer in his *Jeanne d'Arc*. Dreyer spent months seeking the forty actors who constitute the Inquisitors' tribunal. The search for these actors resembled that for stage properties that are hard to come by. Dreyer made every effort to avoid resemblances of age, build, and physiognomy. If the actor thus becomes a stage property, this latter, on the other hand, frequently functions as actor. At least it is not unusual for the film to assign a role to the stage property. Instead of choosing at random from a great wealth of examples, let us concentrate on a particularly convincing one. A clock that is working will always be a disturbance on the stage. There it cannot be permitted its function of measuring time. Even in a naturalistic play, astronomical time would clash with theatrical time. Under these circumstances it is highly revealing that the film can, whenever appropriate use time as measured by a clock. From this more than from many other touches it may clearly be recognized that under certain circumstances each and every prop in a film may assume important functions. From here it is but one step to Pudovkin's statement that "the playing of an actor which is connected with an object and is built around it . . . is always one of the strongest methods of cinematic construction." (W. Pudovkin, *Filmregie und Filmmanuskript*, Berlin, 1928, p. 126.) The film is the first art form capable of demonstrating how matter plays tricks on man. Hence, films can be an excellent means of materialistic representation.

(12) The change noted here in the method of exhibition caused bv mechanical reproduction applies to politics as well. The present crisis of the bourgeois democracies comprises a crisis of the conditions which determine the public presentation of the rulers. Democracies exhibit a member of govemment directly and personally before the nations representatives. Parliament is his public. Since the innovations of camera and recording

equipment make it possible for the orator to become audible and visible to an unlimited number of persons, the presentation of the man of politics before camera and recording equipment becomes paramount. Parliaments, as much as theaters, are deserted. Radio and film not only affect the function of the professional actor but Iikewise the function of those who also exhibit themselves before this mechanical equipment, those who govem. Though their tasks may be different, the change affects equally the actor and the ruler. The trend is toward establishing controllable and transferable skills under certain social conditions. This results in a new selection, a selection before the equipment from which the star and the dictator emerge victorious.

(13) The privileged character of the respective techniques is lost. Aldous Huxley writes:

"Advances in technology have led . . . to vulgarity. . . . Process reproduction and the rotary press have made possible the indefinite multiplication of writing and pictures. Universal education and relatively high wages have created an enormous public who know how to read and can afford to buy reading and pictorial matter. A great industry has been called into existence in order to supply these commodities. Now, artistic talent is a very rare phenomenon; whence it follows . . . that, at every epoch and in all countries, most art has been bad. But the proportion of trash in the total artistic output is greater now than at any other period. That it must be so is a matter of simple arithmetic. The population of Western Europe has a little more than doubled during the last Century. But the amount of reading-and seeing-matter has increased, I should imagine, at least twenty and possibly fifty or even a hundred times. If there were n men of talent in a population of x millions, there will presumably be 2n men of talent among 2x millions. The situation may be summed up thus. For every page of print and pictures published a century ago, twenty or perhaps even a hundred pages are published today. But for every man of talent then living, there are now only two men of talent. It may be of course that, thanks to universal education, many potential talents which in the past would have been stillborn are now enabled to realize themselves. Let us assume, then, that there are now three or even four men of talent to every one of earlier times. It still remains true to say that the consumption of reading-and seeing-matter has far outstripped the natural production of gifted writers and draughtsmen. It is the same with hearing-matter. Prosperity, the gramophone and the radio have created an audience of hearers who consume an amount of hearing- matter that has increased out of all proportion to the increase of population and the consequent natural increase of talented musicians. It follows from all this that in all the arts the output of trash is both absolutely and relatively greater than it was in the past; and that it must remain greater for just so long as the world continues to consume the present inordinate quantities of reading- matter, seeing-matter, and hearing-matter."-Aldous Huxley, *Beyond the Mexique Bay. A Travellers Journal*, London, 1949, pp. 274 ff. First published in 1934.

This mode of observation is obviously not progressive.

(14) The boldness of the cameraman is indeed comparable to that of the surgeon. Luc Durtain lists among specific technical sleights of hand those "which are required in surgery in the case of certain difficult operations. I choose as an example a case from oto-rhinolaryngology; ... the so-called endonasal perspective procedure; or I refer to the acrobatic tricks of larynx surgery which have to be performed following the reversed picture in the laryngoscope. I might also speak of ear surgery which suggests the precision work of watchmakers. What range of the most subtle muscular acrobatics is required from the man who wants to repair or save the human body! We have only to think of the couching of a cataract where there is virtually a debate of steel with nearly fluid tissue, or of the major abdominal operations (laparotomy)."-Luc Durtain, *op. cit.*

(15) This mode of observation may seem crude, but as the great theoretician Leonardo has shown, crude modes of observation may at times be usefully adduced. Leonardo compares painting and music as follows: "Painting is superior to music because, unlike unfortunate music, it does not have to die as soon as it is born. . ..Music which is consumed in the very act of its birth is inferior to painting which the use of varnish has rendered eternal." (Trattato I, 29.)

(16) Renaissance painting offers a revealing analogy to this Situation The incomparable development of this art and its significance rested not least on the integration of a number of new sciences, or at least of new scientific data. Renaissance painting made use of anatomy and perspective, of mathematics, meteorology, and chromatology. Valéry writes: "What could be further from us than the strange claim of a Leonardo to whom painting was a supreme goal and the ultimate demonstration of knowledge? Leonardo was convinced that painting demanded universal knowledge, and he did not even shrink from a theoretical analysis which to us is stunning because of its very depth and precision. . . ."-Paul Valery, *Pièces sur l'art*, "Autour de Corot," Paris, p. 191.

(17) "The work of art," says André Breton, "is valuable only in so far as it is vibrated by the reflexes of the future." Indeed, every developed art form intersects three lines of development. Technology works toward a certain form of art. Before the advent of the film there were photo booklets with pictures which flitted by the onlooker upon pressure of the thumb, thus portraying a boxing bout or a tennis match. Then there were the slot machines in bazaars; their picture sequences were produced by the turning of a crank.

Secondly, the traditional art forms in certain phases of their development strenuously work toward effects which later are effortlessly attained by the new ones. Before the rise of the movie the Dadaists' Performances tried to create an audience reaction which Chaplin later evoked in a more natural way.

Thirdly, unspectacular social changes often promote a change in receptivity which will benefit the new art form. Before the movie had begun to create its public, pictures that were no longer immobile captivated an assembled audience in the so-called *Kaiserpanorama*. Here the public assembled before a screen into which stereoscopes were mounted, one to each beholder. By a mechanical process individual pictures appeared briefly before the stereoscopes, then made way for others. Edison still had to use similar devices in presenting the first movie strip before the film screen and projection were known. This strip was presented to a small public which stared into the apparatus in which the succession of pictures was reeling off. Incidentally, the institution of the *Kaiserpanorama* shows very clearly a dialectic of the development. Shortly before the movie turned the reception of pictures into a collective one, the individual viewing of pictures in these swiftly outmoded establishments came into play once more with an intensity comparable to that of the ancient priest beholding the statue of a divinity in the cella.

(18) The theological archetype of this contemplation is the awareness of being alone with one's God. Such awareness, in the heyday of the bourgeoisie, went to strengthen the freedom to shake off clerical tutelage. During the decline of the bourgeoisie this awareness had to take into account the hidden tendency to withdraw from public affairs those forces which the individual draws upon in his communion with God.

(19) The film is the art form that is in keeping with the increased threat to his life which modern man has to face. Man's need to expose himself to shock effects is his adjustment to the dangers threatening him. The film corresponds to profound changes in the apperceptive apparatus-changes that are experienced on an individual scale by the man in the street in big-city traffic, on a historical scale by every present-day citizen.

(20) As for Dadaism, insights important for Cubism and Futurism are to be gained from the movie. Both appear as deficient attempts of art to accommodate the pervasion of reality by the apparatus. In contrast to the film, these schools did not try to use the apparatus as such for the artistic presentation of reality, but aimed at some sort of alloy in the joint presentation of reality and apparatus. In Cubism, the premonition that this apparatus will be structurally based on optics plays a dominant part; in Futurism, it is the premonition of the effects of this apparatus which are brought out by the rapid sequence of the film strip.

(21) One technical feature is significant here, especially with regard to newsreels, the propagandist importance of which can hardly be overestimated. Mass reproduction is aided especially by the reproduction of masses. In big parades and monster rallies, in sports events, and in war, all of

which nowadays are captured by camera and sound recording, the masses are brought face to face with themselves. This process, whose significance need not be stressed, is intimately connected with the development of the techniques of reproduction and photography. Mass movements are usually discerned more clearly by a camera than by the naked eye. A bird's-eye view best captures gatherings of hundreds of thousands. And even though such a view may be as accessible to the human eye as it is to the camera, the image received by the eye cannot be enlarged the way a negative is enlarged. This means that mass movements, induding war, constitute a form of human behavior which particularly favors mechanical equipment.

The Radio Symphony
An Experiment in Theory (A)
by Theodor W. Adorno

The Problem

To make a study of what radio transmission does musically to a musical structure or to different kinds of music would be a vast undertaking. It involves problems of a great many types and levels, concerning the material and the technicalities of transmission, (B) which can be solved only by the close collaboration of analytically minded musicians, social scientists, and experts on radio engineering. Here would appear the problem of the role played in traditional serious music by the "original"—that is, the live performance one actually experiences, as compared with mass reproduction on the radio. Or one would have to investigate to what extent the technical conditions of jazz in themselves establish a configuration of quasi-mechanized technique with quasi-subjective expression weirdly analogous to that of the actual mechanization of radio transmission with the quasi-expressive ballads with which our radio programs are jammed. Attention must be accorded to chamber music, which structurally is best suited to radio transmission but which, for socio-psychological reasons, is very rarely heard over the air. (C)

It is not our intention to do more than suggest the significance of such problems here. Instead of elaborating them systematically to their fullest extent, we restrict ourselves to one example analyzed in detail, in order to demonstrate concretely the implications as well as the complexity of the field. We are primarily concerned with pointing out the fact that serious music as communicated over the ether may indeed offer optimum conditions for retrogressive tendencies in listening, for the avalanche of fetishism which is overtaking music and burying it under the moraine of entertainment. The statement of the problem and the model analysis which we offer here are in the nature of a challenge to musical and social research. We are undertaking an experiment in theory.

The subject matter of this experiment in theory is the fate of the symphony and, more specifically, of the Beethoven symphony, when it is transmitted by radio. The reasons for this approach are sociological and musical. A typical statement exhibiting official optimism presents claims that today "the farmers' wife in the prairie states listen to great music performed by great artists as they go about their morning housework." (D) The Beethoven symphony is popularly identified with such great music. The truth or falsity of such complacent statements concerning the spreading of great music, however, can be gleaned only be an investigation of a broadcast with the presentation of a live symphony.

The musical reasons for the choice of the symphony as instance become clear in the course of the analysis. Beethoven is selected not only because he is the standard classic of cultural sales talk in music, but also because his music exhibits most clearly some of the features we regard as particularly affected by radio transmission. Earlier symphonic music is less exposed to changes by radio because the problem of sound volume and the issue of dynamic development play a lesser role than in Beethoven; the later romantic symphony is less characteristic because it does not offer the central problem of the radio symphony: the problem of the fate of the "integral form."

Characteristics of the Symphony

Even those who optimistically assume that radio brings great symphonic music to people who never heard it before concede that symphonies brought to the overburdened hypothetical farmer in the Middle West are somewhat affected and deteriorated by radio transmission. But in principle, they maintain that these differences matter only to the musical snobs (E) who know so much about music in general and about symphonic music in particular. The finer shades and differences—so they say—are of no importance to the layman who must flrst become acquainted with the material. Better a symphony that is not quite as good as it is supposed to be in Carnegie Hall, than no symphony at all. Whoever dares to oppose such a view is likely to be regarded as an esthete who has no true sympathy for the needs and desires of the people. Yet the social analyst must risk being castigated as a misanthrope if he is to pursue social essence, as distinct from the facade.

Analysis of a radio symphony must rid itself of the commonsense view that the alterations brought about by radio have no signifikant bearing on the symphonic purpose. To begin with, it must cast off the conventional definition of symphony which asserts that it is merely a sonata for orchestra. (F) For insight into the changes a Beethoven symphony suffers in radio transmission depends upon the specific understanding of symphonic form as it crystallized and maintained itself in the comparatively short period of Haydn, Mozart, and Beethoven. This specific understanding is not furthered by analyzing the symphony in stereotyped terms such as exposition, development, repetition, or even more subtle ones such as the antagonism of the two main subjects of the exposition, (G) their "bridge," their conclusion, the way they develop and undergo their modified recurrence. However easy it may be to identify all those typical constituents of form in every Beethoven symphony, they are essential not abstractly, but only within the interplay of the inexchangeable content of each work. Such schematic identification actually is too easy: any approach starting from the mere recognition of those invariants, tends to deliver listening up to a mechanical process in which any symphony can be replaced by any other which has the same framework.

If reference to those terms does not add much in the actual following of a specific work, it is even less helpful in achieving an understanding of the meaning and function of symphonic form *per se*.

What characterizes a symphony when experienced in immediate listening, as distinct not only from chamber music, but also from orchestral forms such as the suite or the "tone poem," is a particular intensity and concentration. This intensity rests musically upon the incomparably greater density and concision of thematic relationships of the symphonic as against other forms. This density and concision are strictly technical and not merely a by-product of expression. They imply first a complete economy of craft; that is to say, a truly symphonic movement contains nothing fortuitous, every bit is ultimately traceable to very small basic elements, and is deduced from them and not introduced, as it were, from outside, as in romantic music. (H)

Secondly, this economy itself does not reside in a static identity, as in pre-classical music. It is not content with mere repetition, but is intrinsically bound up with variation. If everything in a Beethoven symphony is identical in its ultimate motifical content, nothing is literally identical in the sense of plain repetition, but everything is "different" according to the function it exercises within the development of the whole. A Beethoven symphonic movement is essentially the unity of a manifold as well as the manifoldness of a unity, namely, of the identical thematic material. This interrelationship of perpetual variation is unfolded as a process—never through mere "statement" of detail. It is the most completely organized piece of music that can be achieved. Every detail, however spontaneous in emphasis, is absorbed in the whole by its very spontaneity and gets ist true weight only by its relation to the whole, as revealed finally by the symphonic process. Structurally, one hears the first bar of a Beethoven symphonic movement only at the very moment when one hears the last bar. Romanticism failed to produce symphonic works of this exacting character because the increase in importance of the expressive detail as against the whole, rendered impossible the determination of every moment by the totality. While listening to a typical romantic symphony one remains fully conscious, sometimes all too conscious, (I) of the time it consumes, despite the immensely progressive novelty of the details. With Beethoven it is different. The density of thematic interwovenness, of "antiphonic" work, tends to produce what one might call a suspension of 'time consciousness.'

When a movement like the first of Beethoven's Fifth or Seventh Symphonies, or even a very long one such as the first of the *Eroica* is performed adequately, one has the feeling that the movement does not take seven or fifteen minutes or more, but virtually one moment. It is this very power of symphonic contraction of time which annihilates, for the duration of the adequate performance, the contingencies of the listener's private existence—thus constituting the actual basis of those experiences which, in commentator phraseology, are called the elatedness of an audience as a result of the sublimity of the symphony.

The Role of Sound Intensity

To what extent are the inherent constituents of the Beethoven symphonic form realized by radio?

To start from the most primitive fact about symphonic music: it may be stated in terms of "absolute dynamics", the meaning of which is well known from the visual sphere, particularly from architecture. A cathedral acquires an essential condition of its actual function, as well as its aesthetic meaning, only in proportion to the human body. A model of a cathedral in table size is something totally different from the actual cathedral, not only quantitatively but also qualitatively. On the Campo Santo in Genoa, there is a tomb in the form of a diminutive imitation of the Milan dome. The building itself, which is of highly questionable architectural value, becomes plainly ridiculous in miniature: the impression one has is much like the one reeeived upon seeing the sugar-coated architecture of wedding cakes. The question of absolute dimensions in architecture has its counterpart in music in the question of absolute dynamics.

The power of a symphony to "absorb" its parts into the organized whole depends, in part, upon the sound volume. Only if the sound is "larger," as it were, than the individual so as to enable him to "enter" the door of the sound as he would enter through the door of a cathedral, may he really become aware of the possibility of merging with the totality which structurally does not leave any loophole. The element of being larger may be construed comparatively in terms of the intensity range; that is to say, the intensity range of symphonic sound must be larger, because of the exigencies of symphonic form, than any musical range the individual listener can conceive of producing himself either by singing or playing. (J) Absolute symphonic dimensions, furthermore, carry with them the existence of an experience which it is difficult to render even in rough terms, but which is, nonetheless, fundamental in the apperception of [the] symphony and is the true musical objective of technical discussion of auditory perspective: the experience of symphonic space. To "enter" a symphony means to listen to it not only as to something before one, but as something around one as well, as a medium in which one "lives." It is this surrounding quality that comes closest to the idea of symphonic absorption.

All these qualities are radically affected by radio. The sound is no longer "larger" than the individual. In the private room, that magnitude of sound causes disproportions which the listener mutes down. The "surrounding" function of music also disappears, partly because of the diminutions of absolute dimensions, partly because of the monaural conditions of radio broadcasting. What is left of the symphony even in the ideal case of an adequate reproduction of sound colors, is a mere chamber symphony. (K) If the symphony today reaches masses who have never before been in touch with it, it does so in a way in which their collective aspect and what might he called the collective aspect of the symphony itself, are practically eliminated from the musical pattern—which becomes, as it were, a piece of furniture of the private room.

One must be careful not to derive therefrom a premature judgment on radio, or try to "save" music from it. The abolition of the "surrounding" quality of music on the radio, has its progressive aspects. This "surrounding quality of music is certainly part of music's function as a drug, the criticism of which, inaugurated by Nietzsche and revived by such contemporary writers as Jean Cocteau, is justified and has been considerably furthered by radio. (1) The drug tendency is very clear in Wagner where the mere magnitude of the sound, into whose waves the listener can dive, is one of the means of catching the listeners, quite apart from any specific musical content. In Beethoven, where the musical content is highly articulate, the largeness of the sound does not have this irrational function, but is the more intrinsically connected with the structural devices of the work, and is therefore also the more deeply affected by broadcasting. Paradoxical as it may appear, a Beethoven symphony becomes more problematical as a broadcast than the music of a Wagner opera.

Threat to the Stucture

This may be made clear by such a well-known piece of music as the first movement of the Fifth Symphony. It is characterized by its simplicity. A very short and precise motif, the one with which it opens, is conveyed by an unabating intensity of presentation. Throughout the movement it remains clearly recognizable as the same motif: its rhythm is vigorously maintained. Yet there is no mere repetition, but development: the melodic content of the basic rhythm, that is to say, the intervals which constitute it, change perpetually; it gains structural perspective by wandering from one instrument or instrumental group to another and appearing sometimes in the foreground as a main event, at other times as a mere background and accompaniment. Above all, it is presented in gradations, dynamic developments, the continuity of which is achieved through the identity of the basic material. At the same time, this identity is modified by the different dynamic grades in which the basic motif occurs. Thus the simplicity of the movement is inextricably bound up with an elaborate richness of texture: the richness prevents the simple from becoming primitive, while simplicity prevents richness from dissipation into mere details. It is this unity within the manifold as well as this manifoldness within that unity which constitute the antiphonic work finally terminating in the suspension of time-consciousness. This interrelationship of unity and manifoldness, and not only the loudness of the sound, is itself affected by the dynamic reductions of radio.

First of all, the whole building up of the movement upon the one simple motif—the creation *ex nihilo*, as it were, which is so highly significant in Beethoven—can be made understandable only if the motif, which is actually nothing in itself, is presented in such a way that from the very beginning it is underscored as the substance of everything that is to come. The flrst bars of the Fifth Symphony, if rightly performed, must possess the characteristic of a "statement," of a "positing." This positing characteristic however, can be achieved only by the utmost dynamic intensity. Hence, the question of loudness ceases to be a purely external one and affects the very structure of [the] symphony Presented without the dynamic emphasis which makes out of the Nothing of the first bars virtually the Everything of the total movement, the idea of the work is missed before it has been actually started. The suspension of time-consciousness is endangered from the very beginning: the simple, no longer emphasized in its paradoxical nature as Nothing and Everything, threatens to degenerate into the trite if the "nothingness" of the beginning fails to be absorbed into the whole by the impetus of the statement. The tension is broken and the whole movement is on the verge of relapsing into time.

It is threatened, even more, by the compression of the dynamic range. Only if the motif can develop from the restrained pianissimo to the striking yet affirming fortissimo, is it actually revealed as the "cell" which represents the whole even when exposed as a mere monad. Only within the tension of such a gradation does its repetition become more than repetition. The more the gradation is compressed—which is necessarily the case in radio—the less this tension is felt. Dynamic repetition is replaced by a mere ornamental, tectonic one. The movement loses its character of process and the static repetition becomes purposeless: the material repeated is so simple that it requires no repetition to be understood. Though something of the tension is still preserved by radio, it does not suffice. The Beethoven tension obtains its true significance in the range from Nothing to All. As soon as it is reduced to the medium range between piano and forte, the Beethoven symphony is deprived of the secret of origin as well as the might of unveiling.

It could be argued that all these changes by radio turn the symphony into a work of chamber music which, although different from symphony, has merits of its own. A symphony, conceived in symphonic terms, however, would necessarily become a bad work of chamber music. Its symphonic simplicity would make itself felt as poverty in chamber music texture as lack of polyphonous interwovenness of parts as well as want of extensive melodic lines developed simultaneously. Simplicity would cease to function in the symphonic way. Clearly, a Beethoven symphony played on the piano by four hands, although it is only a one-color reproduction, its to be preferred to a chamber music arrangement, because it still preserves something of the specifically symphonic attack by fingers striking the keys, whereas that value is destroyed by the softened chamber music arrangement which, by virtue of its mere arrangedness, easily approaches the sound of the so-called salon orchestra. Radio symphony bears a stronger resemblance to the chamber music transcription than to the simple yet faithful translation into the mere piano sound. Its colorfulness is as questionable as it would be in a salon arrangement. For the sound colors, too, are affected on the air, and it is through their deterioration that the work becomes bad chamber music. Symphonie richness is distorted no less than symphonic simplicity. While trying to keep the symphonic texture as plain and transparent as possible, Beethoven articulates it by attaching the smallest units of motifical construction to as many different instruments and instrumental groups as possible. These smallest units together form the surface of an outspoken melody, while their coloristic differentation realizes at the same time the construction and all its interrelationships underneath the surface. The finer the shades of motifical interrelationships within the construction, the finer necessarily the shades of changing sound colors. These essential subtleties more than anything else tend to be effaced by radio. While exaggerating conspicuous contrasts, radio's neutralization of sound colors practically blots out precisely those minute differences upon which the classical orchestra is built as against the Wagnerian, which has much larger coloristic means at its disposal.

Richard Stauss, in his edition of Berlioz' *Treatise on Instrumentation*, observes that the second violins-never quite so brilliant and intense as the first violins-are different instruments, so to speak, from the first. (L) Such differences play a decisive part in the Beethoven articulatjon of symphonic texture: a single melody, subdivided between first violins, second violins and violas, becomes plastic according to the instrumemal disposition—that is to say, the elements of the melody which are meant to be decisive are played by the first violins while those intended rather as incidental are played by the second violins or violas. At the same time, their unity is maintained by the fact that they are all strings playing in the same tonal region. Radio achieves only unity, whereas differences such as those between first and second violins are automatically eliminated. Moreover, certain sound colors, like that of the oboe, are changed to such an extent that the instrumental equilibrium is thrown out of joint. All these colors are more than mere means of instrumental make-up, that is, are integral parts of the composition which they as well as the dynamics articulate; their alteration consummates the damage wreaked by radio upon symphonic structure. The less articulate symphony becomes, the more does it lose its character of unity and deteriorate into a conventional and simultaneously slack sequence, consisting of the recurrence of neat tunes whose interrelation is of no import whatever. Thus it becomes ever more apparent why it is Beethoven who falls victim to radio rather than Wagner and late romanticism. For it is in Beethoven that the idea of articulate unity constitutes the essence of the symphonic scheme. That unity is achieved by a severe economy of means forbidding their reduction, which is inevitable by radio.

Trivialization

In the light of the preceding analysis, the hackneyed argument that radio, by bringing symphony to those formerly unfamiliar with it, compensates for its slight alterations, tilts over into its opposite: the less the listeners know the works in their original form, the more is their total impression necessarily erroneously based on the specific radio phenomena delivered to them. And these phenomena are, in addition, far from being structurally consistent. One is tempted to call them contradictory in themselves. A process of polarization sets in through radio transmission of the symphony: it becomes trivialized and romanticized at the same time.

The trivialization of symphony, first of all, is bound up with its relapse into time. The compression of symphonic time is relaxed because the technical prerequisites have been made blunt. The time the radio symphony consumes is the empirical time. It is in ironic keeping with the technical limitations imposed by radio on the live symphony that they are accompanied by the listener's capacity to turn off the music whenever he pleases. He can arbitrarily supersede it—in contrast to the concert hall performance where he is forced, as it were, to obey its laws. It may be questioned whether symphonic elation is really possible or desirable. At any rate, radio expedites its liquidation.

Its very sound tends to undermine the idea of spell, bf uniqueness and of "great music," which are ballyhooed by radio sales talk.

But not only the spell and the high-flown notion of symphonic totality fall victim to mechanization. The decline of the unity, which is the essence of symphony, is concomitant with a decay of the manifold comprehended by it. The symphonic particulars become atoms. The tendency toward atomistic listening obtains its exact and objective technical foundation through radio transmission. (M) The meaning of the music automatically shifts from the totality to the individual moments because their interrelation and articulation by dynamics and colors is no longer fully affected. These moments become semi-independent episodes, organized mainly by their chronological succession.

The symphony has often been compared with the drama. Though this comparison tends to overemphasize the dualistic character, the dialogue aspect of symphony, it must still be admitted that it is justified in so far as symphony aims at an "intensive" totality, an instantaneous focusing of an "idea" rather than an extensive totality of "life" unfolding itself within empirical time. (N) It is in this sense that radio symphony ceases to be a drama and becomes an epical form, or, to make the comparison in less archaic terms, a narrative. And narrative it becomes in an even more literal sense, too. The particular, when chipped off from the unity of symphony, still retains a trace of the unity in which it functioned. A genuine symphonic theme, even if it takes the whole musical stage and seems to be temporarily hypostatized and to desert the rest of the music, is nonetheless of such a kind as to impress upon one that it is actually nothing in itself but basically something "out of" something else. Even in its isolation it bears the mark of the whole. As this whole, however, is not adequately realized in the phenomenon that appears over the air, the theme, or an individual symphonic moment, is presented like something from a context itself blurred or even absent. In other words, through radio, the individual elements of symphony acquire the character of quotation. Radio symphony appears as a medley or potpourri in so far as the musical atoms it offers up acquire the touch of having been picked up somewhere else and put together in a kind of montage. What is heard is not Beethoven's Fifth but merely musical information from and about Beethoven's Fifth. The commentator, in expropriating the listener's own spontaneity of judgment by prating about the marvels of the world's immortal music, is merely the human executor of the trend inherent in music on the air, which, by reassembling fragments from a context not itself in evidence, seems to be continually offering the reassurance: "This is Beethoven's Fifth Symphony." The image character of radio cannot be altogether explained by abstract reference to physical conditions alone, but these conditions must be shown at work on the symphonic structure, wreaking havoc on musical sense.

Quotation Listening

The issue of "quotation" is inseparably bound up with the structure and significance of symphonic themes themselves. Sententious precision which summarizes the meaning of preceding dramatic development or situation, is an age-old ingredient of dramatic structure. The sententious passages, by reflecting upon the action, detach themselves from the immediacy of the action itself. Through this detachment they become reified, emphasized, and facilely quotable. The abstract generality of maxims for practical life into which they translate the concrete idea of the drama brings them close to the banal. At times the sententious moments supersede concrete dramatic sense altogether. There is the revealing joke about elderly ladies who express delight in *Hamlet* with the single reservation that it consists of quotations. In the realm of music radio has realized a similar tendency and has transformed Beethoven's Fifth Symphony into a set of quotations from theme songs.

The symphonic theme of the Beethoven period may structurally very well be compared with the sententious element of the drama. It consists in most cases of the triad. It is based on the triad harmonically and it circumscribes the triad melodically. As the triad is the general principle of major-minor tonality, the triadic theme has a touch of "generality" itself; it is, to a great extent, interchangeable with other triadic themes. The striking similarity between the material of movements as totally different as the finale of Mozart's G Minor Symphony from the scherzo of Beethoven's Fifth, bears witness to this generality. This generality of symphonic theme is balanced by its precision, which is in the main achieved by one short and distinct rhythmical formula apt to be remembered as well as to be repeated. Musical commentators have often compared symphonic themes with mottoes in literature, and German musicology frequently alludes to "head motifs" (*Kopfmotive*) as opening a symphonic movement.

All this points up the sententious character of the symphonic theme. It is this character that offers the theme up to the process of trivialization by radio. The triviality characteristic of live symphonic themes serves a double purpose: that of "generality" transcending the specific case in which they appear, and their existence as a mere material for self-development. Radio interferes with both these purposes. Being atomized, the symphonic theme fails to show its "generality." It calls for significance just as it is. From the viewpoint of consistent symphonic construction it would be possible to imagine a substitute for the famous second theme of the first movement of Schubert's B Minor Symphony—the so-called "Unfinished." The radio listener who does not care much for the movement and waits for the theme would get the shock of his life if it were replaced by another. Moreover, the theme that sticks out because it has lost its dynamic function, can no longer fulfill its truly musical role—which is to serve as a mere material of what follows—as soon as everything that follows is visualized only from the viewpoint of the undeveloped material of the theme. Hence, in the isolation of the symphonic theme, only the trivial remains. And in turn it is the triviality of the symphonic detail which makes it so easy to remember and own it as a commodity under the more general trademark of "culture."

For by sounding like a quotation—the quintessence of the whole—the trivialized theme assumes a peculiar air of authority, which gives it cultural tone. Only what is established and accepted as a standard social value is quoted, and the anxiety of the listeners to recognize the so-called Great Symphonies by their quotable themes is mainly due to their desire to identify themselves with the standards of the accepted and to prove themselves to be small cultural owners within big ownership culture. This tendency again springs from the "electrocution" of symphony by radio, without taking into account radio's social authoritarianism. It has already been mentioned that radio tends to present symphony as a series of results rather than a process. The more a particular result is set off against the process in which it gains creation, the more it ceases to be "the problem" of its own treatment. Within the Symphonie process the theme has its fate. It is "disputed"; by radio the theme becomes definite. In the process of symphonic development it is not conceived as something rigid but fluent, even in its seemingly dogmatic first presentation. By radio even its musically remote transformations sound like themes of their own. If one could say, exaggeratedly, that in symphonic music nothing is theme and everything is development—which holds good literally for some modern symphonic music, particularly for Mahler—one could say as well that by radio everything becomes "theme." The emphasis which every symphonic moment acquires through the radio voice is unlike the emphasis which the symphonic theme possesses in its live "positing." As positing, it owes ist emphasis to the potentiality for process which it contains within itself. By radio it becomes emphasized because that process has been broken through and the theme absolutizes itself in its mere present subsistence, in its being as it is. It is this literal-minded and pharisaical self-righteousness of the theme which transforms it into quotation.

It must be emphasized that the substitution of quotation for reproduction does not mean a greater faithfulness to the original but just the opposite. Quotation is reproduction in its decline. While genuine reproduction would stand in a tension-like relation to its object and realize it by again "producing" it, quotation-reproduction sheds all spontaneity, dissolves all tension toward the object and seizes upon all particulars of the object as fixed and reified items. It is essential to the object, that is, the symphonic original, that it be reproduced in the sense of being produced again rather than of being photographed in degenerated colors and modified proportions. A Beethoven symphony is essentially a process; if that process is replaced by a presentation of frozen items, the performance is faithless even if executed under the battle cry of the utmost fidelity to the letter.

Romanticization

Radio symphony promotes the romanticization of music no less than its trivialization. The authoritarian theme, the "result" replacing the process and thus destroying symphonic spell, acquires a spell of its own. History of symphonic musical production after Beethoven itself reveals a shift from the totality aspect to the detail, which bears a strong resemblance to the shift which the Beethoven symphony suffers through radio. The shift after Beethoven took place in the name of subjective expression. Lyrical expression tends to emphasize the atom and separate it from any comprehensive "objective" order. Radio disintegrates classical music in much the same way as romanticism reacted to it. If radio atomizes and trivializes Beethoven, it simultaneously renders the atoms more "expressive," as it were, than they had been before. The weight which falls upon the isolated detail conveys to it an importance that it never has in its context. And it is this air of importance that makes it seem to "signify" or express something all the time, whereas in the original the expression is mediated by the whole. Consonantly, radio publicity proclaims the "inspiration" of symphonic themes, although precisely in Beethoven the movement, if anything, is inspired and not the theme. It is the romantic notion of melodic inventiveness which radio projects upon dassical music strictly socalled. Details are deified as well as reified.

This has paradoxical consequences. One might expect that radio, since it affects the freshness of sound colors, makes them less conspicuous than in live music. Precisely the opposite is true. Together with the structural totality there vanishes in radio the process of musical spontaneity, of musical "thinking" of the whole by the listener. (The notion of musical thinking refers to everything in musical apperception that goes beyond the mere presence of the sensual stimulus.) The less the radio phenomenon evokes such thinking, the greater is the emphasis on the sensual side as compared with live music, where the sensual qualities are in themselves "better." The structural element of music—the element that is defamed by many listeners as "intellectual" though it constitutes the concreteness of the musical phenomenon even more than the sound—is skipped over, and they content themselves with the stimuli remaining, however shopworn these stimuli may be. In romantic music and even in romantic interpretation of Beethoven, those stimuli actually were the bearers of musical "expression." Deteriorated as they are now, they still maintain something of their romantic glamour. Certain of them today, through the radio, assume such a glamour even though they never had it before, because their institutionalization casts about them a social validity which listeners credit to the music. That is why the atoms, sentimentalized by radio through the combination of triviality and expressiveness, reflect something of the spell which the totality has lost. To be sure, it is not the same spell. It is rather the spell of the commodity whose value is adored by its customers.

In the Symphonic field those works surrender themselves to radio most readily which are conglomerates of tunes of both sensual richness and structural poverty—tunes making unnecessary the process of thinking which is anyhow restrained by the way the phenomenon comes out of the radio set. The preference for Tchaikovsky among radio listeners is as significant a commentary on the inherent nature of the radio voice as on the broader social issues of contemporary listening habits. Moreover, it is very likely that Beethoven is listened to in terms of Tchaikovsky. The thesis that music by radio is no longer quite "serious" implies that radio music already prejudices the capacity to listen in a spontaneous and conscious way. The radio voice does not present the listeners with material adequate to such desiderates. They are forced to passive sensual and emotional acceptance of predigested yet disconnected qualities, whereas those qualities at the same time become mummified and magicized.

Is Symphonic Music "Spread"?

This shows the necessity for starting from the sphere of reproduction of musical works by radio instead of from an analysis of listeners' reactions. The latter presupposes a kind of naive realism with respect to such notions as symphony or "great music" on the air. If that music is fundamentally different from what it is supposed to be, listeners' statements about their reactions to it must be evaluated accordingly. There is no justification for unqualifiedly accepting the listener's word about his sudden delight in a Beethoven symphony, if that symphony is changed the very moment it is broadcast into something closely akin to entertainment. Further, the analysis invalidates the optimistic idea that the knowledge of the deteriorated or even "dissolved" radio symphony may be a first step toward a true, conscious and adequate musical experience. For the way a symphony appears by radio is not "neutral" with regard to the original. It does not convey a hollow one-colored effigy which can be "filled" and made more concrete by later live listening. The radio symphony's relation to the live symphony is not that of the shadow to the robust. Even if it were, the shadow cannot be given flesh by the transfusion of red blood corpuscles. The changes brought about by radio are more than coloristic; that they are changes of the symphony's own essential structure means not only that this structure is not adequately conveyed but that what does come out opposes that structure and constitutes a serious obstacle against its realization. Beethoven's musical sense does not match with the postulates it evokes itself when transmitted on the air. Reference may again be made to the coloristic element. The radio phenomenon produces an attitude in the listener which leads him to seek color and stimulating sounds. Music, however, composed in structural rather than coloristic terms does not satisfy these mechanized claims. The color of a Beethoven symphony in live performance as well as by radio is incomparably less radiant, more subdued not only than those of Wagner, Richard Strauss, or Debussy, but poorer even than the supply of current entertainment. Moreover, the coloristic effects which Beethoven achieves are valid only against the ascetic background of the whole. The cadenza of the oboe in the beginning of the repetition of the first movement of the Fifth Symphony is striking only as a contrast to the bulk of the strings: as a coloristic effect in itself it would be "poor," and it is the misinterpretation of such relations which leads some of today's happy-go-lucky routine musicians, who are nothing but competent, to such ingenuous statements as that Beethoven was not able to score well. If radio, however, brings into the limelight just such particles as the oboe cadenza, may it not actually provoke those opinion Statements and even a resistance within the listeners—a resistance which is only superficially compensated by the official respect for established values—because the symphony fails to satisfy the very same demands which it seems to raise? But the resistance goes beyond unfavorable comparisons between the full seven-course dinner in color of [Paul] Whiteman's rendition of the *Rhapsody in Blue* and the frugal meal of the symphony in black and white consumed, as it were, as a meal merely. The transformation of the symphonic process into a series of results means that the listeners receive the symphony as a ready-made piecemeal product which can be enjoyed with a minimum of effort on his part. Like other ready-made articles, radio symphony tends to make him passive: he wants to get something out of it, perhaps to give himself up to it, but, if possible, to have nothing to do with it, and least of all to "think" it. If it is true that the experience of the actual meaning of symphonic structure implies something like an activity of concrete musical thinking, this thinking is antagonized by radio presentation. It is signifikant that the same listeners who are allegedly overwhelmed by symphonic music are also ever ready to dwell upon what they call their emotions as against what they call "intellectual" in music. For it is as certain that actual musical understanding, by transcending the isolated, sensual moments of music and categorizing them by the interconnection of the past and the coming within the work, is bound to definite intellectual functions, as it is certain that the stubborn and spiteful adherence to one's private emotional sphere tends to build a wall against these experiences—the very experiences by which alone a Beethoven symphony can be properly understood. Great music is not music that sounds the best, and the belief in that sound is apt to tilt over into frank hostility against what, though mediated by the sound, is more than sound. It is highly doubtful if the boy in the subway whistling the main theme of the finale of Brahms's First Symphony actually has been gripped by that music. By the way he picks out that tune he translates it into the language of only a few. It may well be that this translation falls into an historical process, the perspectives of which go far beyond the limits of traditional aesthetics.

If this be true, one should not speak about spreading music while that spreading implies the abnegation of the same concepts of musical classicism, in the name of which serious music is handled by radio. At least no responsible educational attempt can be built directly upon radio symphony without taking into consideration that the radio symphony is not the live symphony and cannot therefore have the same cultural effect as the live symphony. No such educational attempt is worth undertaking that does not give the fullest account of the antagonistic tendencies promulgated by serious music in radio.

- (1941)

Notes

(A) The author wishes to express his indebtedness for editorial assistance to Josef Maier and George Simpson.

(B) Of the related problems, which may very well basically affect the structure and the meaning of broadcast music, we refer only to one: the problem of the hearstripe. Even if the set functions properly, the "current," namely, the thermal noises,can be heard. These continuous noises constitute a hear-stripe. The hear stripe, which of course varies with the quality of the set, tends to disappear from the musical surface as soon as the performance takes shape. But it still can be heard underneath the music. It may not attract any attention and it may not even enter the listener's consciousness; but as an objective characteristic of the phenomenon it plays a part in the apperception of the whole.

One might venture to suggest that the psychological effect of the hear-stripe is somewhat similar to the awareness of the screen in the movies: music appearing upon such a hear-stripe may bear a certain image-like character of its own. Since at the present stage in technical development—particularly by means of FM—this undercurrent of noise is supposed to be abolished, the present study does not take into broader consideration this particular aspect of the field.

(C) The fact that a majority of listeners prefers "symphonic" music to chamber music can be accounted for as follow: (a) the factor of primitive and spectacular strength of sound, its "publicity character"; (b) a multicolored structure is more attractive to the untrained ear than a unicolored one; (c) the specific, symphonic intensity and emphasis, a feature, in which chamber music is more or less lacking; (d) the structure of symphonic music of the "classical" period is often simpler than that of chamber music of the same period. This holds good particularly for the question of polyphony. The texture of classical chamber music is generally more polyphonous than that of symphonies. Polyphony, however, to most listeners is the main obstacle to understanding.

(D) Dixon Skinner, "Music Goes into Mass Production", *Harpers Magazine,* April 1939, p. 487.

(E) Cf. Robert West, S-*o-o-o-o You're Going on the Air!* (New York: Rodin, 1934), p. 56. [The passage Adorno has in mind is the following, pp. 56-57: "A certain class of listeners are loud in protest that the stations and the sponsors stoop to conquer. They demand that every one of the thousands of musical programs shall be exactly suited to their personal taste. They seek perfection in everything as they themselves define perfection.... Cynics need not fear that good music will be hacked to pieces and rendered futile over the air in the approaching years. Were Beethoven to live today to see his exalted vogue, he would no doubt gush with happiness. The Ninth Symphony can be repeated safely without becoming stale. With improvements in sound effects electrically, the audience will receive more than the usual fraction of melodic harmony communicated through the presentday receiver. He will be lifted literally to the skies by orchestral, choral and operatic works, where he today is but stirred to elementary emotion with limited delivery.(rl))"

(F) Cf. Paul Bekker, *The Symphony from Beethoven to Mahler* (Berlin: Schuster and Loeffler, 1918). Paper read before the Frankfurt Main Association for Modern Art, 1918, p. 8. [Adorno gives the title of this sixty-one-page monograph in English; it was in fact only available in German: *Die Sinfonie von Beethoven bis Mahler.* (rl)]

(G) The "dualism" of themes, which is, by most commentators, urged as the main characteristic of the sonata form in general and the symphonic form in particular, actually plays only a minor role in Beethoven. Generally the "second" theme is by no means in marked contrast to the first theme (as it is, for instance, in the first movement of romantic symphonies even as early as Schubert's C Major and B Minor) but is carefully "mediated" with the first theme to avoid any sharp contrast which might endanger the unity of the whole movement. Further, in Beethoven the so-called second theme is very seldom "one" theme but, in most cases, a unity of manifold thematic ingredients so that it is often difficult to identify one particular thematic *Gestalt* as "the" second theme. This is especially apparent in one of Beethoven's most famous symphonic pieces, the first movement of the Ninth Symphony. The replacement of the actual Beethoven symphony by patterns of late romanticism is reflected even in the way in which musical commentators talk about it: they mistake it for Tchaikovsky.

(H) Extreme examples of this characteristic are evident in some few works of Beethoven in which the first and second themes are actually identical and only presented in a different mode, as in the first movement of the *Appassionata*. Such cases are exceptions, but only in the sense that they bring to the fore a tendency which operates to one degree or another latently throughout Beethoven s mature works. The identity of the basic motifical [sic] content of apparently widely divergent themes of a Beethoven movement can be demonstrated in a less obvious yet striking example—the *Waldstein* Sonata. Here the character of the second theme, in E major—its "cantability"—is actually very different from the character of the first theme in C major—its quick pulsation. Yet the second theme is based upon an "inversion" of the intervals of the first theme, within the space of a fifth. One may characterize this technique in Beethoven as that of universal variation. In later composers this technique has been employed only by Brahms and by the Schoenberg School to any large extent.

(I) The famous slogan about Schubert's "heavenly lengths" applies to this fact.

(J) This largeness of sound has nothing to do with noisiness, but simply with the necessity for enclosing the listener. It is not a matter of loudness but of a wide range between minimum and maximum sound.

(K) Here, as in innumerable other cases, radio is an executor of musical and social tendencies which have developed extraneous to it. In musical production itself, independent of radio, the form of chamber symphony and other hybrids between orchestra and chamber music, have gained an ever-increasing importance since Schoenberg's *Kammer- symphonie* (1906). Whatever the merits of this development for composition itself, the transformation of a Beethoven symphony into a *Kammersymphonie* by radio certainly undermines what is conventionally regarded as a main asset of radio transmission, namely, its seemingly collective message. It is hard to reconcile the experience of collectivity with that of "chamber." The German musicologist, Paul Bekker, went so far as to define symphony its collective message, by its community-building power.* Obviously, this theory loses its point when the situation of symphony listeners becomes one of complete atomization, such as symbolized by millions of individuals scattered among their various "chambers," at the same time as the symphony [that] they get is a chamber symphony. [* This discussion appears in Bekker, *Die Sinfonie von Beethoven bis Mahler*; with regard to Beethoven, see especially pp. 22-28, 31-32. (rl)]

(L)   Hector Berlioz, *Instrumentalionslehre*, ed. Richard Strauss, 2 vols. (Leipzig: C. F. Peters, 1905), vol. I, p. 64.

(M)   This tendency is perhaps the most universal of present-day listening on the sheerly musical level. It is furthered by features as divergent as musical recognition contests that put chief emphasis on the isolated detail, the "theme," just as books that tell the reader how to memorize the main tunes of famous symphonies by subjecting them to certain words, and the standardization of popular music where the whole is so stereotyped that only the detail fetches the listener's attention.

(N)   Cf. Georg Lukàcs, *The Theory of the Novel* (Berlin: Paul Cassirer, 1920), p. 31. [Adorno gives the title in English; the edition cited was in fact published in German: *Die Theorie des Romans: Ein geschichtsphilosophischer Versuch über die Formen der grossen Epik.*(rl)]

Note by Richard Leppert

Adorno wrote this essay in English. Occasionally, he failed to catch typos (such as "life" for "live" in reference to musical performances, in the first and third paragraphs; and "form" when he intended "from"). In a few instances he simply misspelled words. I have corrected these errors and also have changed his occasional use of British orthography to American.

Adorno's punctuation is sometimes incorrect, in particular as regards misplaced commas that confuse the reader or distorted meaning; I have corrected these mistakes. Finally, Adorno liked to employ a comma and dash together (a practice common to his written German, even in instances where conventional practice—which differs in this regard from English—would not require it). I have retained whichever one of the two marks that seemed best to fit the context.

(1) Friedrich Nietzsche, *The Birth of Tragedy*, in *The Birth of Tragedy and the Case of Wagner*, trans. Walter Kaufmann (New York: Vintage, 1967), p. 25: "Contemporary *German music*, which is romanticism through and through and most un-Greek of all possible art forms—moreover, a first-rate poison for the nerves, [is] doubly dangerous among a people who love drink and who honor lack of clarity as a virtue, for it has the double quality of a narcotic that both intoxicates and spreads a *fog*." The passage is from section 6 of the "Attempt at Self-Criticism," added to the text in 1886, hence following his break with Wagner as the text bitingly reflects. *The Birth of Tragedy* (1872) was Nietzsche's first book. Jean Cocteau's (1889-1963) opium addiction is detailed in his *Opium: The Diary of a Cure*, trans. Margaret Crosland and Sinclair Road (London: Peter Owen, 1957); the text is a set of notes written in 1929 with additions made the following year when the book was at proof stage. It indudes a variety of references to modern music. Cocteau's *A Call to Order*, trans. Rollo H. Myers (London: Faber and Gwyer, 1926), based on texts written between 1918 and 1926, indudes the brief *Cock and Harlequin*, first published separately in 1918, consisting of aphorisms on art in general

and music in particular, by Bach, Beethoven, Wagner, Bizet, Saint-Saens, Musorgsky, Puccini, Debussy, Satie, Strauss, Stravinsky, and Schoenberg, among others. Cocteau's allusion to music as a drug comes in a short section concerning Nietzsche and Wagner and, obviously, replicates Nietzsche's position: "There are certain long works which are short. Wagner's works are long works which are long, and *longdrawn-out*, because this old sorcerer looked upon boredom as a useful drug for the stupefaction of the faithful" (p. 14). The *Cock and Harlequin* was something of an aesthetic manifesto for modern French music, and notably for Les Six (Auric, Durey, Honegger, Milhaud, Poulenc, and Tailleferre). Cocteau wrote in specific Opposition to German music, as evident, for example, in his comment on Schoenberg: "Schoenberg is a master; all our musicians, as well as Stravinsky, owe something to him, but Schoenberg is essentially a blackboard musician" (p. 15). In particular, Cocteau writes at length about, and with great admiration of, Satie, whose early career he actively and successfully promoted. The text also induces laudatory comments about music by various of Les Six composers as well as Stravinsky.

The Grain of the Voice
by Roland Barthes

Language, according to Benveniste, is the onlv semiotic System capable of *interpreting* another semiotic system (though undoubtedly there exist limit works in the course of which a system feigns self-interpretation - *The Art of the Fugue*). How, then, does language manage when it has to interpret music? Alas, it seems, very badly. If one looks at the normal practice of music criticism (or, which is often the same thing, of conversations 'on' music), it can readily be seen that a work (or its performance) is only ever translated the poorest of linguistic categories: the adjective. Music, by natural bent, is that which at once receives an adjective. The adjective is inevitable: this music is this, this execution is that. No doubt the moment we turn an art into a subject (for an article, for a conversation) there is nothing left but to give it predicates; in the case of music, however, such predication unfailingly takes the most facile and trivial form, that of the epithet. Naturally, this epithet, to which we are constantly led by weakness or fascination (little parlour game: talk about a piece of music without using a single adjective), has an economic function: the predicate is always the bulwark with which the subject's imaginary protects itself from the loss which threatens it The man who provides himself or is provided with an adjective is now hurt, now pleased, but always *constituted.* There is an imaginary in music whose function is to reassure, to constitute the subject hearing it (would it be that music is dangerous - the old Platonic idea? that music is an access to *jouissance*, to loss, as numerous ethnographic and populär examples would tend to show?) and this imaginary immediately comes to language via the adjective. A historical dossier ought to be assembled here, for adjectival criticism (or predicative interpretation) has taken on over the centuries certain institutional aspects. The musical adjective becomes legal whenever an *ethos* of music is postulated,

each time, that is, that music is attributed a regular - natural or magical
- mode of signification. Thus with the ancient Greeks, for whom it was
the musical *language* (and not the contingent work) in its denotative
structure which was immediately adjectival, each mode being linked to
a coded expression (rude, austere, proud, virile, solemn, majestic,
warlike, educative, noble, sumptuous, doleful, modest, dissolute,
voluptuous); thus with the Romantics, from Schumann to Debussy,
who substitute for, or add to, the simple indication of tempo (*allegro,
presto, andante*) poetic, emotive predicates which are increasingly
refined and which are given in the national language so as to diminish
the mark of the code and develop the 'free' character of the predication
(*sehr kräftig, sehr präcis, spirituel et discret*, etc.).

Are we condemned to the adjective ? Are we reduced to the
dilemma of either the predicable or the ineffable? To ascertain whether
there are (verbal) means for talking about music without adjectives, it
would be necessary to look at more or less the whole of music
criticism, something which I believe has never been done and which,
nevertheless, I have neither the intention nor the means of doing here.
This much, however, can be said: it is not by struggling against the
adjective (diverting the adjective you find on the tip of the tongue
towards some substantive or verbal periphrasis) that one stands a
chance of exorcising music commentary and liberating it from the
fatality of predication; rather than trying to change directly the
language on music, it would be better to change the musical object
itself, as it presents itself to discourse, better to alter its level of
perception or intellection, to displace the fringe of contact between
music and language.

It is this displacement that I want to outline, not with regard
to the whole of music but simply to a part of vocal music (*lied* or
melodie): the very precise space (genre) of *the encounter between a
language and a voice*. I shall straightaway give a name to this signifier
at the level of which, I believe, the temptation of ethos can be
liquidated (and thus the adjective banished): the *grain*, the grain of the

voice when the latter is in a dual posture, a dual production - of language and of music.

What I shall attempt to say of the 'grain' will, of course, be only the apparently abstract side, the impossible account of an individual thrill that I constantly experience in listening to singing. In order to disengage this 'grain' from the acknowledged values of vocal music, I shall use a twofold opposition: theoretical, between the pheno-text and the geno-text (borrowing from Julia Kristeva), and paradigmatic, between two singers, one of whom I like very much (although he is no longer heard), the other very little (although one hears no one but him), Panzera and Fischer- Dieskau (here merely ciphers: I am not deifying the first or attacking the second).

Listen to a Russian bass (a church bass - opera is a genre in which the voice has gone over in its entirety to dramatic expressivity, a voice with a grain which little signifies): something is there, manifest and stubborn (one hears only *that*), beyond (or before) the meaning of the words, their form (the litany), the melisma, and even the style of execution: something which is directly the cantor's body, brought to your ears in one and the same movement from deep down in the cavities, the muscles, the membranes, the cartilages, and from deep down in the Slavonic language, as though a single skin lined the inner flesh of the performer and the music he sings. The voice is not personal: it expresses nothing of the cantor, of his soul; it is not original (all Russian cantors have roughly the same voice), and at the same time it is individual: it has us hear a body which has no civil identity, no 'personality', but which is nevertheless a separate body. Above all, this voice bears along *directly* the symbolic, over the intelligible, the expressive: here, thrown in front of us like a packet, is the Father, his phallic stature. The 'grain' is that: the materiality of the body speaking its mother tongue; perhaps the letter, almost certainly *signifiance*.

Thus we can see in song (pending the extension of this distinction to the whole of music) the two texts described by Julia

Kristeva. The *pheno-song* (if the transposition be allowed) covers all the phenomena, all the features which belong to the structure of the language being sung, the rules of the genre, the coded form of the melisma, the composer's idiolect, the style of the interpretation: in short, everything in the performance which is in the service of communication, representation, expression, everything which it is customary to talk about, which forms the tissue of cultural values (the matter of acknowledged tastes, of fashions, of critical commentaries), which takes its bearing directly on the ideological alibis of a period ('subjectivity', 'expressivity', 'dramaticism', 'personality' of the artist). The *geno-song* is the volume of the singing and speaking voice, the space where significations germinate 'from within language and in its very materiality'; it forms a signifying play having nothing to do with communication, representation (of feelings), expression; it is that apex (or that depth) of production where the melody really works at the language - not at what it says, but the voluptuousness of its sounds-signifiers, of its letters - where melody explores how the language works and identifies with that work. It is, in a very simple word but which must be taken seriously, the *diction* of the language.

From the point of view of the pheno-song, Fischer- Dieskau is assuredly an artist beyond reproach: everything in the (semantic and lyrical) structure is respected and yet nothing seduces, nothing sways us to *jouissance*. His art is inordinately expressive (the diction is dramatic, the pauses the checkings and releasings of breath, occur like shudders of passion) and hence never exceeds culture: here it is the soul which accompanies the song, not the body What is difficult is for the body to accompany the musical diction not with a movement of emotion but with a 'gesture-support'; (1)   all the more so since the whole of musical pedagogy teaches not the culture of the 'grain' of the voice but the emotive modes of its delivery - the myth of respiration How many singing teachers have we not heard prophesying that the art of vocal music rested entirely on the mastery the correct discipline of breathing! The breath is the *pneuma* the soul swelling or breaking, and any exclusive art of breathing is likely to be a secretly mystical art (a mysticism levelled down to the measure of the long-playing record). The lung, a stupid organ (lights for cats!), swells but gets no erection; it is in the throat, place where the phonic metal hardens and is segmented, in the mask that *signifiance* explodes, bringing not the soul but *jouissance*. With FD, I seem only to hear the lungs, never the tongue the glottis, the teeth, the mucous membranes, the nose. All of Panzera's art, on the contrary, was in the letters, not in the bellows (simple technical feature: you never heard him breathe but only divide up the phrase). An extreme rigour of thought regulated the prosody of the enunciation and the phonic economy of the French language; prejudices (generally stemming from oratorical and ecclesiastical diction) were overthrown. With regard to the consonants, too readily thought to constitute the very armature of our language (which is not, however, a Semitic one) and always prescribed as needing to be 'articulated', detached, emphasized in *order to fulfil the clarity of meaning*, Panzera recommended that in many cases they be *patinated*, given the wear of a language that had been living, functioning, and working for ages past, that they be made simply the springboard for the admirable vowels. There lay the 'truth' of language - not its functionality (clarity, expressivity, communication) - and the range of vowels received all the *signifiance* (which is meaning in its potential voluptuousness): the opposition of *é* and *è* (so necessary in conjugation), the purity - almost electronic, so much was its sound tightened, raised, exposed, held - of the most French of vowels, the *ü* (a vowel not derived by French from Latin). Similarly, Panzera carried his *r's* beyond the norms of the singer - without denying those norms. His *r* was of course rolled, as in every classic art of singing, but the roll had nothing peasant-like or Canadian about it; it was an artificial roll, the paradoxical state of a letter-sound at once totally abstract (by its metallic brevity of vibration) and totally material (by its manifest deep-rootedness in the action of the throat). This phonetics - am I alone in perceiving it? am I hearing voices within the voice? but isn't it the truth of the voice to be hallucinated? isn't the entire space of the voice an infinite one? which was doubtless the meaning of Saussure's work on anagrams - does not exhaust *signifiance* (which is inexhaustible) but it does at least hold in check the attempts at expressive reduction operated by a whole culture against the poem and its melody.

It would not be too difficult to date that culture, to define it historically. FD now reigns more or less unchallenged over the recording of vocal music; he has recorded everything If you like Schubert but not FD, then Schubert is today *forbidden* you - an example of that positive censorship (censorship by repletion) which characterizes mass culture though it is never criticized. His art - expressive, dramatic *sentimentally* clear, borne by a voice lacking in any 'grain" in signifying weight, fits well with the demands of an *average* culture. Such a culture, defined by the growth of the number of listeners and the disappearance of practitioners (no more amateurs), wants art, wants music provided they be clear, that they 'translate' an emotion and represent a signified (the 'meaning' of a poem); an art that innoculates pleasure (by reducing it to a known coded emotion) and reconciles the subject to what in music *can be said*: what is said about it, predicatively by Institution, Criticism, Opinion. Panzera does not belong to this culture (he could not have done, having sung before the coming of the microgroove record; moreover I doubt whether, were he singing today, his art would be recognized or even simply *perceived*); his reign, very great between the wars, was that of an exclusively bourgeois art (an art that is, in no way petit-bourgeois) nearing the end of its inner development and, by a familiar distortion, separated from History. It is perhaps, precisely and less paradoxically than it seems, because this art was already marginal mandarin, that it was able to bear traces of *signifiance* to escape the tyranny of meaning.

The 'grain' of the voice is not - or is not merely - its timbre; the *signifiance* it opens cannot better be defined indeed than by the very friction between the music and something else, which something else is the particular language (and nowise the message). The song must speak must write - for what is produced at the level of the geno-song is finally writing. This sung writing of language is as I see it, what the French *mélodie* sometimes tried to accomplish. I am well aware that the German *lied* was intimately bound up with the German language via the Romantic poem, that the poetical culture of Schumann was immense and that this same Schumann used to say of Schubert that had he lived into old age he would have set the whole of German literature to music, but I think nevertheless that the historical meaning of the *lied* must be sought in the music (if only because of its popular origins). By contrast, the historical meaning of the *mélodie* is a certain culture of the French language. As we know, the Romantic poetry of France is more oratorical than textual; what the poetry could not accomplish on its own, however, the *mélodie* has occasionally accomplished with it, working at the language through the poem. Such a work (in the specificity here acknowledged it) is not to be seen in the general run of the *mélodies* produced which are too accommodating towards minor poets, the model of the petit-bourgeois romance, and salon usages, but in some few pieces it is indisputable - anthologically (a little by chance) in certain songs by Fauré and Duparc, massively in the later (prosodic) Fauré and the vocal work of Debussy (even if *Pelléas* is often sung badly - dramatically). What is engaged in these works is, much more than a musical style, a practical reflection (if one may put it like that) on the language; there is a progressive movement from the language to the poem, from the poem to the song and from the song to its performance. Which means that the *mélodie* has little to do with the history of music and much with the theory of the text. Here again, the signifier must be redistributed.

Compare two sung deaths, both of them famous: that of Boris and that of Mélisande. Whatever Mussorgsky's intentions, the death of Boris is *expressive* or, if preferred, *hysterical*; it is overloaded with historical, affective contents. Performances of the death cannot be but dramatic: it is the triumph of the pheno-text, the smothering of *signifiance* under the soul as signified. Mélisande, on the contrary, only dies *prosodically*. Two extremes are joined, woven together: the perfect intelligibility of the denotation and the pure prosodic segmentation of the enunciation; between the two a salutary gap (filled out in Boris) - the *pathos*, that is to say, according to Aristotle (why not?), passion *such as men speak and imagine it*, the accepted idea of death, *endoxical* death. Mélisande dies *without any noise* (understanding the term in its cybernetic sense): nothing occurs to interfere with the signifier and there is thus no compulsion to redundance; simply, the production of a music-language with the function of preventing the singer from being expressive. As with the Russian bass, the symbolic (the death) is thrown immediately (without mediation) before us (this to forestall the stock idea which has it that what is not expressive can only be cold and intellectual; Mélisande's death is 'moving', which means that it shifts something in the chain of the signifier).

The *mélodie* disappeared - sank to the bottom - for a good many reasons, or at least the disappearance took on a good many aspects. Doubtless it succumbed to its salon image, this being a little the ridiculous form of its class origin. Mass 'good' music (records, radio) has left it behind, preferring either the more pathetic orchestra (success of Mahler) or less bourgeois instruments than the piano (harpsichord, trumpet). Above all, however, the death of the *mélodie* goes along with a much wider historical phenomenon to a large extent unconnected to the history of music or of musical taste: the French are abandoning their language, not, assuredly, as a normative set of noble values (clarity, elegance, correctness) - or at least this does not bother me very much for these are institutional values - but as a space of pleasure, of thrill, a site where language works for nothing, that is, in perversion (remember here the singularity - the solitude - of *Lois* by Philippe Sollers, theatre of the return of the prosodic and metrical work of the language).

The 'grain' is the body in the voice as it sings, the hand as it writes, the limb as it performs. If I perceive the 'grain' in a piece of music and accord this 'grain' a theoretical value (the emergence of the text in the work), I inevitably set up a new scheme of evaluation which

will certainly be individual - I am determined to listen to my relation
with the body of the man or woman singing or playing and that
relation is erotic - but in no way 'subjective' (it is not the psychological
'subject' in me who is listening; the climactic pleasure hoped for is not
going to reinforce - to express - that subject but, on the contrary, to
lose it). The evaluation will be made outside of any law, outplaying
not only the law of culture but equally that of anticulture, developing
beyond the subject all the value hidden behind 'I like' or 'I don't like'.
Singers especially will be ranged in what may be called, since it is a
matter of my choosing without there being any reciprocal choice of
me, two prostitutional categories. Thus I shall freely extol such and
such a performer, little-known, minor, forgotten, dead perhaps, and
turn away from such another, an acknowledged star (let us refrain from
examples, no doubt of merely biographical significance); I shall extend
my choice across all the genres of vocal music including popular
music, where I shall have no difficulty in rediscovering the distinction
between the pheno-song and the geno-song (some popular singers
have a 'grain' while others, however famous, do not). What is more,
leaving aside the voice, the 'grain' - or the lack of it - persists in
instrumental music; if the latter no longer has language to lay open
signifiance in all its volume, at least there is the performer's body
which again forces me to evaluation. I shall not judge a performance
according to the rules of interpretation, the constraints of style (any
way highly illusory), which almost all belong to the phenol-song (I
shall not wax lyrical concerning the 'rigour', the 'brilliance', the
'warmth', the 'respect for what is written', etc.), but according to the
image of the body (the figure) given me. I can hear with certainty - the
certainty of the body, of thrill - that the harpsichord playing of Wanda
Landowska comes from her inner body and not from the petty digital
scramble of so many harpsichordists (so much so that it is a different
instrument). As for piano music, I know at once which part of the body
is playing - if it is the arm, too often, alas, muscled like a dancer's
calves, the clutch of the finger-tips (despite the sweeping flourishes of
the wrists), or if on the contrary it is the only erotic part of a pianist's

body, the pad of the fingers whose 'grain' is so rarely heard (it is hardly necessary to recall that today, under the pressure of the mass long-playing record, there seems to be a flattening out of technique; which is paradoxical in that the various manners of playing are all flattened out *into perfection*: nothing is left but pheno-text).

This discussion has been limited to 'classical music'. It goes without saying, however, that the simple consideration of 'grain' in music could lead to a different history of music from the one we know now (which is purely pheno-textual). Were we to succeed in refining a certain 'aesthetics' of musical pleasure, then doubtless we would attach less importance to the formidable break in tonality accomplished by modernity.

Notes

(1) 'Which is why the best way to read me is to accompany the reading with certain appropriate bodily movements. Against non-spoken writing, against non-written speech. For the gesture-support.' Philippe Sollers, *Lois*, Paris 1972, p. 108.

Source: *The Grain of the Voice: 'Le grain de la voix'*, *Musique en jeu 9*, 1972

The Phonograph:
The Toy that Shrank the National Chest
by Marshall Mcluhan

The phonograph, which owes its origin to the electrical telegraph and the telephone, had not manifested its basically electric form and function until the tape recorder released it from its mechanical trappings. That the world of sound is essentially a unified field of instant relationships lends it a near resemblance to the world of electromagnetic waves. This fact brought the phonograph and radio into early association.

Just how obliquely the phonograph was at first received is indicated in the observation of John Philip Sousa, the brass band director and composer. He commented: "With the phonograph vocal exercises will be out of vogue! Then what of the national throat? Will it not weaken? What of the national chest? Will it not shrink?"

One fact Sousa had grasped: The phonograph is an extension and amplification of the voice that may well have diminished individual vocal activity, much as the car had reduced pedestrian activity.

Like the radio that it still provides with program content, the phonograph is a hot medium. Without it, the twentieth century as the era of tango, ragtime, and jazz would have had a different rhythm. But the phonograph was involved in many misconceptions, as one of its early names-gramophone-implies. It was conceived as a form of auditory writing (*gramma*-letters). It was also called "graphophone," with the needle in the role of pen. The idea of it as a "talking machine" was especially popular. Edison was delayed in his approach to the solution of its problems by considering it at flrst as a "telephone repeater"; that is, a storehouse of data from the telephone, enabling the telephone to "provide invaluable records, instead of being the recipient of momentary and fleeting communication." These words of Edison, published in the *North American Review* of June, 1878, illustrate how the then recent telephone invention already had the power to color thinking in other fields. So, the record player had to be seen as a kind of phonetic record of telephone conversation. Hence, the names "phonograph" and "gramophone."

Behind the immediate popularity of the phonograph was the entire electric implosion that gave such new stress and importance to actual speech rhythms in music, poetry, and dance alike. Yet the phonograph was a machine merely. It did not at flrst use an electric motor or circuit. But in providing a mechanical extension of the human voice and the new ragtime melodies, the phonograph was propelled into a central place by some of the major currents of the age. The fact of acceptance of a new phrase, or a speech form, or a dance rhythm is already direct evidence of some actual development to which it is significantly related. Take, for example, the shift of English into an interrogative mood, since the arrival of "How about that?" Nothing could induce people to begin suddenly to use such a phrase over and over, unless there were some new stress, rhythm, or nuance in interpersonal relations that gave it relevance.

It was while handling paper tape, impressed by Morse Code dots and dashes, that Edison noticed the sound given off when the tape moved at high speed resembled "human talk heard indistinctly." It then occurred to him that indented tape could record a telephone message. Edison became aware of the limits of lineality and the sterility of specialism as soon as he entered the electric field. "Look," he said, "it's like this. I start here with the intention of reaching here in an experiment, say, to increase the speed of the Atlantic cable; but when I've arrived part way in my straight line, I meet with a phenomenon, and it leads me off in another direction and develops into a phonograph." Nothing could more dramatically express the turning point from mechanical explosion to electrical implosion. Edison's own career embodied that very change in our world, and he himself was often caught in the confusion between the two forms of procedure.

It was just at the end of the nineteenth century that the psychologist Lipps revealed by a kind of electric audiograph that the single dang of a bell was an intensive manifold containing all possible symphonies. It was somewhat on the same lines that Edison approached his problems. Practical experience had taught him that embryonically all problems contained all answers when one could discover a means of rendering them explicit. In his own case, his determination to give the phonograph, like the telephone, a direct practical use in business procedures led to his neglect of the instrument as a means of entertainment. Failure to foresee the phonograph as a means of entertainment was really a failure to grasp the meaning of the electric revolution in general. In our time we are reconciled to the phonograph as a toy and a solace; but press, radio, and TV have also acquired the same dimension of entertainment. Meantime, entertainment pushed to an extreme becomes the main form of business and politics. Electric media, because of their total "field" character, tend to eliminate the fragmented specialties of form and function that we have long accepted as the heritage of alphabet, printing, and mechanization. The brief and compressed history of the phonograph includes all phases of the written, the printed, and the mechanized word. It was the advent of the electric tape recorder that only a few years ago released the phonograph from its temporary involvement in mechanical culture. Tape and the Lp. record suddenly made the phonograph a means of access to all the music and speech of the world.

Before turning to the l.p. and tape-recording revolution, we should note that the earlier period of mechanical recording and sound reproduction had one large factor in common with the silent picture. The early phonograph produced a brisk and raucous experience not unlike that of a Mack Sennett movie. But the undercurrent of mechanical music is strangely sad. It was the genius of Charles Chaplin to have captured for film this sagging quality of a deep blues, and to have overlaid it with jaunty jive and bounce. The poets and painters and musicians of the later nineteenth century all insist on a sort of metaphysical melancholy as latent in the great industrial world of the metropolis. The Pierrot figure is as crucial in the poetry of Laforgue as it is in the art of Picasso or the music of Satie. Is not the mechanical at its best a remarkable approximation to the organic? And is not a great industrial civilization able to produce anything in abundance for everybody? The answer is "Yes." But Chaplin and the Pierrot poets and painters and musicians pushed this logic all the way to reach the image of Cyrano de Bergerac, who was the greatest lover of all, but who was never permitted the return of his love. This weird image of Cyrano, the unloved and unlovable lover, was caught up in the phonograph cult of the blues. Perhaps it is misleading to try to derive the origin of the blues from Negro folk music; however, Constant Lambert, English conductor-composer, in his *Music Ho!*, provides an account of the blues that preceded the jazz of the post-World War I. He concludes that the great flowering of jazz in the twenties was a popular response to the highbrow richness and orchestral subdety of the Debussy- Delius period. Jazz would seem to be an effective bridge between highbrow and lowbrow music, much as Chaplin made a similar bridge for pictorial art. Literary people eagerly accepted these bridges, and Joyce got Chaplin into *Ulysses* as Bloom, just as Eliot got jazz into the rhythms of his early poems.

Chaplin's clown-Cyrano is as much a part of a deep melancholy as Laforgue's or Satie's Pierrot art. Is it not inherent in the very triumph of the mechanical and its omission of the human? Could the mechanical reach a higher level than the talking machine with its mime of voice and dance? Do not T. S. Eliot's famous lines about the typist of the jazz age capture the entire pathos of the age of Chaplin and the ragtime blues?

> When lovely woman stoops to folly and
> Paces about her room again, alone,
> She smoothes her hair with automatic hand,
> And puts a record on the gramophone.

Read as a Chaplin-like comedy, Eliot's Prufrock makes ready sense. Prufrock is the complete Pierrot, the little puppet of the mechanical civilization that was about to do a flip into its electric phase.

It would be difficult to exaggerate the importance of complex mechanical forms such as film and phonograph as the prelude to the automation of human song and dance. As this automation of human voice and gesture had approached perfection, so the human work force approached automation. Now in the electric age the assembly line with its human hands disappears, and electric automation brings about a withdrawal of the work force from industry. Instead of being automated themselves-fragmented in task and function-as had been the tendency under mechanization, men in the electric age move increasingly to involvement in diverse jobs simultaneously, and to the work of learning, and to the programming of computers.

This revolutionary logic inherent in the electric age was made fairly clear in the early electric forms of telegraph and telephone that inspired the "talking machine." These new forms that did so much to recover the vocal, auditory, and mimetic world that had been repressed by the printed word, also inspired the strange new rhythms of "the jazz age," the various forms of syncopation and symbolist discontinuity that, like relativity and quantum physics, heralded the end of the Gutenberg era with its smooth, uniform lines of type and organization.

The word "jazz" comes from the French *jaser*, to chatter. Jazz is, indeed, a form of dialogue among instrumentalists and dancers alike. Thus it seemed to make an abrupt break with the homogeneous and repetitive rhythms of the smooth waltz. In the age of Napoleon and Lord Byron, when the waltz was a new form, it was greeted as a barbaric fulfillment of the Rousseauistic dream of the noble savage. Grotesque as this idea now appears, it is really a most valuable clue to the dawning mechanical age. The impersonal choral-dancing of the older, courdy pattern was abandoned when the waltzers held each other in a personal embrace. The waltz is precise, mechanical, and military, as its history manifests. For a waltz to yield its full meaning, there must be military dress. "There was a sound of revelry by night" was how Lord Byron referred to the waltzing before Walterloo. To the eighteenth century and to the age of Napoleon, the citizen armies seemed to be an individualistic release from the feudal framework of courtly hierarchies. Hence the association of waltz with noble savage, meaning no more than freedom from status and hierarchic deference. The waltzers were all uniform and equal, having free movement in any part of the hall. That this was the Romantic idea of the life of the noble savage now seems odd, but the Romantics knew as little about real savages as they did about assembly lines.

In our own century the arrival of jazz and ragtime was also heralded as the invasion of the bottom-wagging native. The indignant tended to appeal from jazz to the beauty of the mechanical and repetitive waltz that had once been greeted as pure native dancing. If jazz is considered as a break with mechanism in the direction of the discontinuous, the participant, the spontaneous and improvisational, it can also be seen as a return to a sort of oral poetry in which performance is both creation and composition. It is a truism among jazz performers that recorded jazz is "as stale as yesterday's newspaper." Jazz is alive, like conversation; and like conversation it depends upon a repertory of available themes. But performance is composition. Such performance insures maximal participation among players and dancers alike. Put in this way, it becomes obvious at once that jazz belongs in that family of mosaic structures that reappeared in the Western world with the wire services. It belongs with symbolism in poetry, and with the many allied forms in painting and in music.

The bond between the phonograph and song and dance is no less deep than its earlier relation to telegraph and telephone. With the first printing of musical scores in the sixteenth Century, words and music drifted apart. The separate virtuosity of voice and instruments became the basis of the great musical developments of the eighteenth and nineteenth centuries. The same kind of fragmentation and specialism in the arts and sciences made possible mammoth results in industry and in military enterprise, and in massive cooperative enterprises such as the newspaper and the symphony orchestra.

Certainly the phonograph as a product of industrial, assemblyline organization and distribution showed little of the electric qualities that had inspired its growth in the mind of Edison. There were prophets who could foresee the great day when the phonograph would aid medicine by providing a medical means of discrimination between "the sob of hysteria and the sigh of melancholia . . . the ring of whooping cough and the hack of the consumptive. It will be an expert in insanity, distinguishing between the laugh of the maniac and drivel of the idiot. . . . It will accomplish this feat in the anteroom, while the physician is busying himself with his last patient." In practice, however, the phonograph stayed with the voices of the Signor Foghornis, the basso-tenores, robusto-profundos.

Recording facilities did not presume to touch anything so subtle as an orchestra until after the First War. Long before this, one enthusiast looked to the record to rival the photograph album and to hasten the happy day when "future generations will be able to condense within the space of twenty minutes a tone-picture of a single lifetime: five minutes of a child's prattle, five of the boy's exultations, five of the man's reflections, and five from the feeble utterances of the deathbed." James Joyce, somewhat later, did better. He made *Finnegans Wake* a tone poem that condensed in a single sentence all the prattlings, exultations, observations, and remorse of the entire human race. He could not have conceived this work in any other age than the one that produced the phonograph and the radio.

It was radio that finally injected a full electric charge into the world of the phonograph. The radio receiver of 1924 was already superior in sound quality, and soon began to depress the phonograph and record business. Eventually, radio restored the record business by extending popular taste in the direction of the classics.

The real break came after the Second War with the availability of the tape recorder. This meant the end of the incision recording and its attendant surface noise. In 1949 the era of electric hi-fi was another rescuer of the phonograph business. The hi-fi quest for "realistic sound" soon merged with the TV image as part of the recovery of tactile experience. For the sensation of having the performing instruments "right in the room with you" is a striving toward the union of the audile and tactile in a finesse of fiddles that is in large degree the sculptural experience. To be in the presence of performing musicians is to experience their touch and handling of instruments as tactile and kinetic, not just as resonant. So it can be said that hi-fi is not any quest for abstract effects of sound in separation from the other senses. With hi-fi, the phonograph meets the TV tactile challenge.

Stereo sound, a further development, is "all-around" or "wrap-around" sound. Previously sound had emanated from a single point in accordance with the bias of visual culture with its fixed point of view. The hi-fi changeover was really for music what cubism had been for painting, and what symbolism had been for literature; namely, the acceptance of multiple facets and planes in a single experience. Another way to put it is to say that stereo is sound in depth, as TV is the visual in depth.

Perhaps it is not very contradictory that when a medium becomes a means of depth experience the old categories of "classical" and "popular" or of "highbrow" and "lowbrow" no longer obtain. Watching a blue-baby heart operation on TV is an experience that will fit none of the categories. When l.p. and hi-fi and stereo arrived, a depth approach to musical experience also came in. Everybody lost his inhibitions about "highbrow," and the serious people lost their qualms about popular music and culture. Anything that is approached in depth acquires as much interest as the greatest matters. Because "depth" means "in interrelation", not in isolation. Depth means insight, not point of view; and insight is a kind of mental involvement in process that makes the content of the item seen quite secondary. Consciousness itself is an inclusive process not at all dependent on content. Consciousness does not postulate consciousness of anything in particular.

With regard to jazz, l.p. brought many changes, such as the cult of "real cool drool," because the greatly increased length of a single side of a disk meant that the jazz band could really have a long and casual chat among its instruments. The repertory of the 1920s was revived and given new depth and complexity by this new means. But the tape recorder in combination with l.p. revolutionized the repertory of classical music. Just as tape meant the new study of spoken rather than written languages, so it brought in the entire musical culture of many centuries and countries. Where before there had been a narrow selection from periods and composers, the tape recorder, combined with l.p., gave a full musical spectrum that made the sixteenth Century as available as the nineteenth, and Chinese folk song as accessible as the Hungarian.

A brief summary of technological events relating to the phonograph might go this way:

The telegraph translated writing into sound, a fact directly related to the origin of both the telephone and phonograph. With the telegraph, the only walls left are the vernacular walls that the photograph and movie and wirephoto overleap so easily. The electrification of writing was almost as big a step into the non-visual and auditory space as the later Steps soon taken by telephone, radio, and TV.

The telephone: speech without walls.
The phonograph: music hall without walls.
The photograph: museum without walls.
The electric light: space without walls.
The movie, radio, and TV: classroom without walls.

Man the food-gatherer reappears incongruously as information- gatherer. In this role, electronic man is no less a nomad than his paleolithic ancestors.

The Future of Music
by John Cage

For many years I've noticed that music-as an activity separated from the rest of life-doesn't enter my mind. Strictly musical questions are no longer serious questions.

It wasn't always that way. When I was setting out to devote my life to music, there still were battles to win within the field of music. People distinguished between musical sounds and noises. I followed Varese and fought for noises. Other musicians also did. In the early thirties the only piece for percussion alone was Varese's *Ionisation*. By 1942 there were over one hundred such works. Now they are countless. Almost anyone who listens to sound now listens easily no matter what overtone structures the sounds have. We no longer discriminate against noises.

We can also hear any pitch, whether or not it's part of a scale of one temperament or another, occidental or oriental. Sounds formerly considered out of tune are now called microtones. They are part and parcel of modern music.

Some people still object to loud sounds. They're afraid of hurting their ears. Once I had the opportunity to hear a very loud sound (the conclusion of a Zaj performance). I'd been in the audience the evening before. I knew when the sound was coming. I moved close to the loudspeaker from which it was to be heard and sat there for an hour, turning first one ear and then the other toward it. When it stopped, my ears were ringing. The ringing continued through the night, through the next day, and through the next night. Early the following day I made an appointment with an ear specialist. On my way to his office, the ringing seemed to have more or less subsided. The doctor made a thorough examination, said my ears were normal. The disturbance had been temporary. My attitude toward loud sounds has not changed. I shall listen to them whenever I get the chance, keeping perhaps a proper distance.

Our experience of time has changed. We notice brief events that formerly might have escaped our notice and we enjoy very long ones, ones having lengths that would have been considered, say fifteen years ago, intolerable.

Nor are we concerned about how a sound begins, continues, and dies away. During a panel discussion on piano music from the People's Republic of China, Chou Wen-Chung said that Western musicians formerly insisted that a pitched sound should stay on pitch, not waver from the moment it begins until it ends. Chinese musicians, he said, feel some change in its course in its pitch enlivens a sound, makes it "musical." Nowadays, anyone listens to any sounds, no matter how flexible or inflexible they are with respect to any of their characteristics. We've become attentive to sounds we've never heard before. I was fascinated when Lejaren Hiller described his project to use Computer means to make a "fantastic orchestra," to synthesize extraordinary sounds, sounds beginning as though plucked, continuing as from pipes, ending as though bowed.

We're also open-minded about silence. Silence isn't as generally upsetting as it used to be.

And melody. *Klangfarbenmelodie* has not taken the place of *bel canto*. It has extended our realization of what can happen. The same is true of aperiodic rhythm: it includes the possibility of periodic rhythm. Two or more lines composed of sounds can be heard whether they involve known or invented kinds of counterpoint or are just simultaneous (not intervallically controlled). Even if two melodies, one very loud, the other very soft, are played at the same time, we know if we listen carefully, or from another position in space, we'll hear them both.

We can be extremely careful about harmony, as Lou Harrison, La Monte Young, and Ben Johnston are, or we can be, as I often am, extremely careless about harmony. Or we can make do as our orchestras do with grey compromise about which sounds sounded together are harmonious.

Anything goes. However, not everything is attempted. Take the division of a whole into parts. In the 'thirties I was impressed by Schoenberg's insistence on musical structure, but disagreed with his view that tonality was its necessary means. I investigated time-lengths as a more comprehensive means. Using permutation, I made tables of the numbers one through twelve, giving their division into prime numbers. These numberseries could be understood either in terms of tonality or time-length or rhythmic structures. The series 1-2-1, which appears in the table for the number 4, can be recognized as an A-B-A structure. It could be expressed tonally or rhythmically (or both). The number 7 has 64 different number-series. Only three of these are A-B-A, namely, 2-3-2, 3-1-3, and 1-5-1. Though some of the others have been exemplified musically, I think many have not. The possibilities increase for the higher numbers. There are 2,048 for the number 12. If we add the possibility of fractions, who knows what musical structures may be discovered? Interesting ones are being found by Elliott Carter and Conlon Nancarrow involving superimposed independent gradual transitions from one tempo to another; those by Nancarrow are particularly interesting. Dealing exclusively with player pianos, he produces extremes of speed that are astonishing and exhilarating.

Many composers no longer make musical structures. Instead they set processes going. A structure is like a piece of furniture, whereas a process is like the weather. In the case of a table, the beginning and end of the whole and each of its parts are known. In the case of weather, though we notice changes in it, we have no clear knowledge of its beginning or ending. At a given moment, we are when we are. The nowmoment.

Were a limit to be set to possible musical processes, a process outside that limit would surely be discovered. Since processes can include objects (be analogous, that is, to environment), we see there is no limit. For some time now, I have preferred processes to objects for just this reason: processes do not exclude objects. It doesn't work the other way around. Within each object, of course, a lively molecular process is in operation. But if we are to hear it, we must isolate the object in a special chamber. To focus attention, one must ignore all the rest of creation. We have a history of doing precisely that. In changing our minds, therefore, we look for that attitude that is nonexclusive, that can include what we know together with what we do not yet imagine.

There is the question of feelings, whether like emotions they seem to come spontaneously from within, or, like likes and dislikes, they seem to be caused by sense perceptions. In either case, we know that life's more fully lived when we are open to whatever-that life is minimized when we protect ourselves from it. Naturally, we don't set out to kill ourselves. We will continue to "wrestle with the Daimonic" (as M. C. Richards puts it), and a variety of disciplines will continue to be used to open the mind to events beyond its control. But more and more a concern with personal feelings of individuals, even the enlightenment of individuals, will be seen in the larger context of society. We know how to suffer or control our emotions. If not, advice is available. There is a cure for tragedy. The path to self-knowledge has been mapped out by psychiatry, by oriental philosophy, mythology, occult thought, anthroposophy, and astrology. We know all we need to know about Oedipus, Prometheus, and Hamlet. What we are learning is how to be convivial. "Here Comes Everybody." Though the doors will always remain open for the musical expression of personal feelings, what will more and more come through is the expression of the pleasures of conviviality (as in the music of Terry Riley, Steve Reich, and Philip Glass). And beyond that a nonintentional expressivity, a being together of sounds and people (where sounds are sounds and people are people). A walk, so to speak, in the woods of music, or in the world itself.

The difference between closed-mindedness and open-mindedness resembles the difference between the critical and creative faculties, or the difference between information about something (or knowledge even) and that something itself. Christian Wolff found the following, written by Charles Ives, and sent it on to me: "What music

is and is to be may be somewhere in the belief of an unknown
philosopher of half a century ago who said, 'How can there be any bad
music? All music is from heaven. If there is anything bad in it, I put it
there-by my implications and limitations. Nature builds the mountains
and meadows and man puts in the fences and labels.'" The fences have
come down and the labels are being removed. An up-to-date aquarium
has all the fish swimming together in one huge tank.

Musical open-mindedness has come about in this century in
Europe both West and East, in the Americas, in Japan, Australia, and
perhaps New Zealand. It doesn't exist, except perhaps exceptionally, in
India, Indonesia, and Africa. (When in traveling around the world with
the Dance Company in 1964 we came to India, Merce Cunningham
said, "This is the land of the future.") Musical open-mindedness exists
in Russia but is not permitted exportation. It is politically excluded in
China (though I've heard tell that sometime in the 'sixties Italy's
representatives in China managed to arrange a concert in Peking of the
music of Sylvano Bussotti).

The reasons for this musical open-mindedness are several.
First of all: the activities, the battles won, by many composers. In this
country alone, open-mindedness is implied by the work particularly of
Ives, Ruggles, Cowell, and Varese. Cowell used to tell the story about
Ruggles and the Florida class in harmony. The problem of modulating
from one key to another "very distant" one was discussed. After an
hour, the instructor asked Ruggles how he, Ruggles, would solve the
problem. Ruggles said: I wouldn't make a problem out of it; I'd just go
from one to the other without any transition.

A second reason for open-mindedness: changes in technology
associated with music. Given the tape recorders, synthesizers, sound
Systems, and computers we have, we could not reasonably have been
expected to keep our minds fixed on the music of earlier centuries,
even though many of the schools, conservatories, and music critics still
do. A third reason for open-mindedness: the interpenetration of
cultures formerly separated. In the nineteenth century even
Englishmen occupying India were few and far between who took

Indian music seriously. Times have changed. At the present time, if a university takes music seriously, it does as Wesleyan University in Connecticut does: it brings together in one school as many different musical cultures of the world as it can afford (music of Africa, of India, of Indonesia, and Japan, together with European music, music of the American Indians, and new electronic music). A fourth reason for openmindedness: there are more of us and we have many ways of getting together (the telephone, the media, travel by air). If one of us doesn't have an idea that will open the minds of the rest of us, another will. We begin to be keenly aware of the richness and uniqueness of each individual and the natural capacity in each person to open up new possibilities for another. In her recent book, *The Crossing Point*, M. C. Richards tells of her work with retarded children, how it is characterized not just by her helping them, but also by their helping her. Some years ago I was asked to speak to a group of doctors associated with a mental hospital in Connecticut. I had no clear idea in my mind what to say. But as I went down the corridors toward the room where I was to speak, I found myself among people "out of their minds." What had to be said to the doctors became clear: You're sitting on top of a gold mine! Share the wealth with the rest of us! The same is true of our prisons. When Buckminster Fuller did not know whether his wife Anne was to live or not (following an automobile accident), or, if she did live, whether she would be incapacitated or not, it was a letter from a former convict in a California penitentiary on the subject of life, love, and death that gave him consolation. There are untouched resources in children and teen-agers which we do not have because we send them to school; and among the military whom we lose by sending them around the world and beneath its surface to bomb-proof offensive installations; and among the senior citizens whom we have persuaded to leave us in favor of sunshine, fun, and games. We have systematically deprived ourselves of all these people, probably because we didn't want them to bother us while we were doing whatever we were doing. But if there is any experience more than another which conduces to open-mindedness, it is the experience of being bothered by another, of being interrupted by another. "We are studying being interrupted." Say we do not practice any spiritual discipline. The telephone then does it for us. It opens us to the world "outside."

George Herbert Mead said that when one is very young he feels he belongs to one family, not to any other. As he grows older, he belongs to one neighborhood rather than another: later, to one nation rather than another. When he feels no limit to that to which he belongs, he has, Mead said, developed the religious spirit. The open-mindedness among composers (which has affected performers and listeners too) is comparable and kin to the religious spirit. The religious spirit must now become social so that all Mankind is seen as Family, Earth as Home. Music's ancient purpose-to sober and quiet the mind, thus making it susceptible to divine influences-is now to be practiced in relation to the Mind of which through technological extension we all are part, a Mind, these days, confused, disturbed, and split.

Music has already taken steps in this direction, toward social interaction, the nonpolitical togetherness of people.

The Renaissance-honored distinctions between composers, performers, and listeners are no longer everywhere maintained. The blurring of these distinctions has come about for several reasons. First of all: the activities of many composers, particularly Feldman and Wolff, who have made their compositions indeterminate, so that performers, rather than merely doing what they are told to do, have the opportunity to use their own faculties, to make decisions in a field of possibilities, to cooperate, that is, in a particular musical undertaking. Those listening to indeterminate music have been encouraged in their listening, since they have been joined in such music by the composers and performers too.

Secondly, technology has brought about the blurring of the distinctions between composers, performers, and listeners. Just as anyone feels himself capable of taking a photograph by means of a camera, so now and increasingly so in the future anyone, using recording and/or electronic means, feels and will increasingly feel himself capable of making a piece of music, combining in his one person the formerly distinct activities of composer, performer, and listener. However, to combine in one person these several activities is, in effect, to remove from music its social nature. It is the social nature of music, the practice in it of using a number of people doing different things to make it, that distinguishes it from the visual arts, draws it toward theater, and makes it relevant to society, even society outside musical society. The popularity of recordings is unfortunate, not only for musical reasons, but for social reasons: it permits the listener to isolate himself from other people. What is needed is not that the several activities of different people come together in one person, but that the distinctions between the roles of different people be blurred, so that they themselves may come together.

A third cause for the blurring of the distinctions between composers, performers, and listeners: the interpenetration of cultures formerly separated. There is no longer an essential difference between some serious music and some popular music-or, you may say, a bridge exists between them: their common use of the same sound systems, the same microphones, amplifiers, and loudspeakers. In the cases of much popular and some oriental musics, the distinctions between composers and performers were never very clear. Notation, as Busoni said it did, did not stand between musician and music. People simply came together and made music. Improvisation. It can take place, so to speak, strictly as within the *raga* and *tala* limitations of Indian music, or it can take place freely, merely in a space of time, as sounds do environmentally, whether in the country or in the cities. Just as aperiodic rhythm can include periodic rhythm, just as process can include object, so free improvisations can include strict ones, can even include compositions. The Jam Session. The Musicircus.

In 1974 Richard K. Winslow suggested changing my instrumental parts for *Etcetera* so that they would read Bowed Instrument, Wind Instrument, Double Reed Single Reed, rather than Violin, Flute, Oboe, Clarinet, thus bringing to parts for pitched instruments something of the vagueness and freedom conventionally given to parts for percussion players. (If you don t have the percussion instrument called for, you substitute something else.) Oriental and occidental instruments together in ensemble. A duet between tuba and sitar! This is possible only when the actions to be made are not on the ground Special to either, but on the ground common to both. Since *Etcetera* I have written *Score with Parts: Twelve Haiku and Renga*, graphic notations in which the parts are differentiated only by numbers. A given part may be played on any instrument.

With our increase in population there has come about a great increase in musical activity. Formerly concerts of new music were few and far between. Now there is more going on than you can shake a stick at. So that it always surprises me when I run into the thought there's nothing further, nothing new, to do in music; though I remember feeling that way in the early 'thirties: I was full of admiration for what had been accomplished; I had not yet gotten to work. For the most part, music that's now being made in New York, the new music, that is, is music I want to hear, though too often I cannot for I'm busy elsewhere. Audiences are large, generally filling the spaces used. And more and more, as in the evenings in New York known as "Sounds out of Silent Spaces," evenings with a cooperative music-making group founded by Philip Corner, the audiences themselves participate.

We can say that this blurring of the distinctions between composers, performers, and listeners is evidence of an ongoing change in society, not only in the structure of society, but in the feelings that people have for one another. Fear, guilt, and greed associated with hierarchical societies are giving way to mutual confidence, a sense of common well-being, and a desire to share with another whatever one person happens to have or to do. However, these changed social feelings which characterize many evenings of new music do not characterize the society as a whole.

Revolution remains our proper concern. But instead of planning it, or stopping what we're doing in order to do it, it may be that we are at all times in it. I quote from M. C. Richards' book, *The Crossing Point*: "Instead of revolution being considered exclusively as an attack from outside upon an established form, it is being considered as a potential resource-an art of transformation voluntarily undertaken from within. Revolution arm in arm with evolution, creating a balance which is neither rigid nor explosive. Perhaps we will learn to relinquish voluntarily our patterns of power and subservience, and work together for organic change."

At the beginning of the *Essay on Civil Disobedience*, Thoreau has this quotation: "That government is best which governs not at all." He adds: "And when men are prepared for it, that will be the kind of government which they will have." Many musicians are ready. We now have many musical examples of the practicality of anarchy. Music with indeterminate parts, no fixed relation of them (no score). Music without notation. Our rehearsals are not conducted. We use that time to make our setups: to make sure that everything that is needed by any of the musicians is there, that everything is in good working order. Musicians can do without government. Like ripe fruit (I refer to the metaphor at the end of Thoreau's *Essay*), they have dropped away from the tree.

Less anarchic kinds of music give examples of less anarchic states of society. The masterpieces of Western music exemplify monarchies and dictatorships. Composer and conductor: king and prime minister. By making musical situations which are analogies to desirable social circumstances which we do not yet have, we make music suggestive and relevant to the serious questions which face Mankind.

Some politically concerned composers do not so much exemplify in their work the desired changes in society as they use their music as propaganda for such changes or as criticism of the society as it continues insufficiently changed. This necessitates the use of words. Sounds by themselves do not put messages across. And when they do not use words, politically concerned composers tend to revert to nineteenth-century musical practices. This is enforced in both Russia and China. And encouraged in England by Cornelius Cardew and the members of the Scratch Orchestra. They study the pronouncements on art by Mao Tse-tung and apply them as literally and legalistically as they can. They therefore have criticized the politically concerned music of Frederick Rjewski and Christian Wolff, simply because new ways to make music have been discovered by both of these composers. Rjewski's works (and some of Garrett List's, too) flow like the rapids of a river: they suggest irresistible change. Rjewski and List have found virtuosi who vocalize rapidly and over long periods of time uninterruptedly (not seeming to take any time off to breathe); Wolff's works invariably reveal to both performers and listeners energy resources they have of which they hadn't been aware and put those energies intelligently to work.

Implicit in the use of words (when messages are put across) are training, government, enforcement, and finally the military. Thoreau said that hearing a sentence he heard feet marching. Syntax. N. O. Brown told me, is the arrangement of the army. The pen has formerly been considered more powerful than the sword. American shame and spiritual frustration result at least in part from the fact that even though the country's best pens and best voices throughout our history have been raised in protest against our government's actions, and even though thorough plans have been clearly proposed for the improvement of environment and the well-being of all people-not just Americans, but all people-the American powers that be remain deaf and blind. We know from Buckminster Fuller and many others that the continued use of fossil fuels is against both environment and the lives of people in it. We should use above-earth energy sources exclusively: sun, wind, tides, and algae. The nations don't seem to know this. National and international triumphs, whether of the USA or other countries, still have to do with the foolish exploitation of below-earth resources. Fuller did not smile when I asked him about atomic energy. Inevitable in it is the slow but steady raising of Earth s temperature to a heat in which life would be unendurable (see Robert L. Heilbroner: *An Inquiry into the Human Prospect*). Since words, when they communicate, have no effect it dawns on us that we need a society in which communication is not practiced, m which words become nonsense as they do between lovers, in which words become what they originally were: trees and stars and the rest of primeval environment. The demilitarization of language: a serious musical concern.

When I was commissioned by the Boston Symphony Orchestra to write a work in celebration of the American Bicentennial, Seiji Ozawa said, "Make it easy!" Our institutions not just the musical ones, are incapable of hard work. Time is counted to the second and limited. The goal of an individual within an Institution has nothing to do with the work to be done or with the State of his mind. It has to do with the payment to be received. A necessary aspect of the immediate future, not just in the field of environmental recovery, is work, hard work, and no end to it. Much of my music since 1974 is extremely difficult to play (the *Etudes Australes* for the pianist Grete Sultan; the *Freeman Etudes* for the Violinist Paul Zukofsky). The overcoming of difficulties. Doing the impossible. Grete Sultan was enthusiastic at the prospect of work. When I told the composer Garrett List what I was up to, there was liveliness in his eyes and a smile or recognition. He also was at work on something having the nature of work. And a recent long work by Christian Wolff is called *Exercises*.

Tom Howell at the University of Illinois inspired his students to explore the playing of two or more notes at a time on a single wind instrument. In the books you can play only one at a time: His teaching produced work. Multiphonics.

As a pianist David Tudor laboriously developed the ability, not yet approached by others to give each attack in a rapid succession of many its own dynamic character. He took the principle underlying *Klangfarbenmelodie* (a succession of different timbres) and applied it to the relation between himself and his instrument: differences of energy of distance and speed of attack, an extension of the understanding of the mechanism of keys, hammers, strings. Nowadays, Tudor rarely plays the piano. His work is in the field of electronics, often in relation to video, and often in collaboration with others He invents components and sound Systems of great originality. He solders and constructs them. He keeps abreast of the developments throughout the world in the field of electronics. He makes new loudspeakers free of the constriction of high fidelity.

There is endless work to be done in the field of electronic music. And many people at work- David Behrman, Gordon Mumma, Robert Ashley, Alvin Lucier, Phill Niblock, to name five. And in the field of video and visual technology (composers also have eyes): Lowell Cross Tony Martin, Nam June Paik, to name three. And in the field of Computer music (shortly everyone, whether he's a musician or not, will have a computer in his pocket): Joel Chadabe, Giuseppe Englaert, Jean-Claude Risset, Lejaren Hiller, Max Mathews, John Chowning, Charles Dodge, Emmanuel Ghent, to name eight

As I look back over my own work, I observe that more often than not I have had other people in mind. I had Robert Fizdale and Arthur Gold in mind when I wrote the *Book of Music for Two Pianos*. The *Sonatas and Interludes* for prepared piano is a portrait of Maro Ajemian. Beginning with my *Music of Changes*, and continuing through *Variations VI*, my music always had David Tudor in mind. I notice now that many composers in their work have not a person but a place (environment) in mind. This is true of Pauline Oliveros' work, *In Memoriam Nikola Tesla*. The concern with place characterizes the work of Alison Knowles, whether she is working with Yoshimasa Wada or Annea Lockwood. Music becomes something to visit. Or a shrine, as in the *Eternal Music* of La Monte Young. An environment to go through (as in a work by Maryanne Amacher, or Max Neuhaus, or Liz Phillips). At Wesleyan University I met two young men studying with Alvin Lucier, Ron Goldman and Nicolas Collins. They gave an electronic concert in the tunnels below the new Arts Center in Middletown. By walking through the tunnels one passed through nodes and noticed (as one does in Oliveros' work) sympathetic vibrations arising in the building and its furniture. There's music to be made in geodesic domes, on unused subway platforms, in laundromats, in fields, forests, and in cities conceived as Robert Moran conceives them as immense concert halls.

Sympathetic vibrations. Suggestiveness and work. I have heard electronic components go into Operation even though they were not plugged into the System. I said to someone who understood electronics and who was helping me, "Don't you think that's strange? It's not connected but it's working." His comment: "It's so close to the others, I would find it stranger if it didn't start working."

People and places. Musical theater. The Happening. The longest one we've ever had (Watergate) is still going on (at least in our minds). It is comparable to Greek or Noh drama. I attended a very short happening (not more than two minutes). It was performed in the window of a coffee shop in Soho by Ralston Farina, a young man who changed his name when he noticed two boxes of cereal. The audience with coats on stood in the street outside. His work was enigmatic and invigorating.

People and places: ritual. People and places: food. I remember attending a Potlatch near Anacortes, Washington. For days and nights people under the same roof sleeping, eating, cooking, dancing, singing. Changing the USA so that it becomes American Indian again. Margaret Mead. Bob Wilson. Jerome Rothenberg. David McAllester. Avery Jimerson of the Seneca Tribe.

Buckminster Fuller's *Synergetics* (876 pages) was published in 1975. It is no doubt inspiring a new music.

Merce Cunningham's dancing is also inspiring. Through the years Cunningham's faithfulness to the principle of work has never wavered. His dance technique itself is not fixed. It is a continuing series of discoveries of what a human body can do when it moves in and through Space. Sometimes he appears as someone who has an insatiable appetite for dance; at other times he seems like dance's slave. James Rosenberg, a young Berkeley, California, poet whose work I admire, makes of himself, as I advised him, a slave to poetry. He is inspired, as I am, by Jackson MacLow's example of untiring devotion. I recall a performance by Charlemagne Palestine that was reminiscent of the body-art of Vito Acconci. Palestine shouted a vocal music at high amplitude while continuously running at high speed through the audience for a long time up to the point of physical exhaustion.

The first part of a new text by Norman O. Brown is on work. It was his reaction, I believe, to the somewhat complacent, though religious, spirit of the young in California communes. The willingness to settle for survival. Brown's concern is how to make a new civilization. Work is the first chapter. Ideas are in the air. In our polluted air there is the idea that we must get to work. Somehow, recently, in New York and in other cities too, the air seems less polluted than it was. Work has begun.

For a musical work to be implemented in China, it must be proposed not by an individual but by a team. The necessity for teamwork in music has been emphasized by Pierre Boulez in a Canadian interview with him about the research institute, IRCAM, now formed at the Centre Pompidou in Paris. The evenings with Philip Corner, Emily Derr, Andrew Franck, Dan Goode, William Hellerman, Tom Johnson, Alison Knowles, Dika Newlin, Carole Weber, Julie Winter, and the participatihg "audience" are team work. They are learning how to work together without one person's telling another what to do, and these evenings are open to strangers. How many people can work together happily, not just efficiently-happily and unselfishly? A serious question which the future of music will help to answer.

When I received the announcement of the evenings with Philip Corner and his friends, I noticed that no names were given, not even Philip Corner's. However, the announcement was not typeset; it was handwritten. And I recognized Philip Corner's handwriting. The omission of names. Anonymity. People going Underground. In order, like Duchamp, to get the work done that is to be done.

People frequently ask me what my definition of music is. This is it. It is work. That is my conclusion.

However, just as I wrote it, the doorbell rang. It was the postman bringing me a present from William McNaughton, his editing of *Chinese Literature* (an anthology from the earliest times to the present day). The book includes many of McNaughton's own translations. On the endpaper of my copy is a dedication to me followed by fourteen Chinese characters, a reference to page 121, and McNaughton's signature. I turned to page 121 and read the following from his translation of *Chuang-tzu's* Book: "Everybody knows that useful is useful, but nobody knows that useless is useful, too." This is from Chapter 4 of *Chuang-tzu's* Book. A tree is described that gives a great deal of shade. It was very old and had never been cut down simply because its wood was considered to be of no use to anyone.

I want to tell the story of Thoreau and his setting fire to the woods. I think it is relevant to the practice of music in the present world situation, and it may suggest actions to be taken as we move into the future.

First of all, he didn't mean to set the fire. (He was broiling fish he had caught.) Once it was beyond his control, he ran over two miles unsuccessfully for help. Since there was nothing he could do alone he walked to Fair Haven Cliff, climbed to the highest rock, and sat down upon it to observe the progress of the flames. It was a glorious spectacle and he was the only one there to see it. From that height he heard bells in the village sounding alarm. Until then he had felt guilty, but knowing that help was coming his attitude changed. He said to himself: "Who are these men who are said to be the owners of these woods, and how am I related to them? I have set fire to the forest, but I have done nothing wrong therein, and it is as if the lightning had done it. These flames are but consuming their natural food."

When the townsmen arrived to fight the fire, Thoreau joined them. It took several hours to subdue the flames. Over one hundred acres were burned. Thoreau noticed that the villagers were generally elated, thankful for the opportunity that had given them so much sport. The only unhappy one.s were those whose property had been destroyed. However, one of the owners was obliged to ask Thoreau the shortest way home, even though the path went through the owner's own land.

Subsequently, Thoreau met a fellow who was poor, miserable, often drunk, worth- less (a burden to society). However, more than any other, this fellow was skillful in the burning of brush. Observing his methods and adding his own insights, Thoreau set down a procedure for successfully fighting fires. He also listened to the music a fire makes, roaring and crackling: "You sometimes hear it on a small scale in the log on the hearth."

Having heard the music fire makes and having discussed his fire-fighting method with one of his friends, Thoreau went farther: suggesting that along with firemen there be a band of musicians playing instruments to revive the energies of weary firemen and to cheer up those who were not yet exhausted.

Finally he said that fire is not only disadvantage. "It is without doubt an advantage on the whole. It sweeps and ventilates the forest floor, and makes it clear and clean. It is nature's broom.... Thus, in the course of two or three years new huckleberry fields are created for birds and for men."

Emerson said that Thoreau could have been a great leader of men, but that he ended up simply as the captain of huckleberry-picking-parties for children. But Thoreau's writing determined the actions of Martin Luther King, Jr., and Gandhi, and the Danes in their light-hearted resistance to Hitler's invasion. India. Nonviolence.

The useless tree that gave so much shade. The usefulness of the useless is good news for artists. For art serves no material purpose. It has to do with changing minds and spirits. The minds and spirits of people are changing. Not only in New York, but everywhere. It is time to give a concert of modern music in Africa. The change is not disruptive. It is cheerful.

This text is a revision of an earlier one finished in 1974 which was given as a lecture at the YMHA in New York City and printed in *Numus West*, No. 5-74.

A Thousand Plateaus / Excerpt from "1837: Of the Refrain"
by Gilles Deleuze & Felix Guattari

The assemblage no longer confronts the forces of chaos, it no longer uses the forces of the earth or the people to deepen itself but instead opens onto the forces of the Cosmos. All this seems extremely general, and somewhat Hegelian, testifying to an absolute Spirit. Yet it is, should be, a question of technique, exclusively a question of technique. The essential relation is no longer matters-forms (or substances-attributes); neither is it the continuous development of form and the continuous variation of matter. It is now a direct relation *material-forces*. A material is a molecularized matter, which must accordingly "harness" forces; these forces are necessarily forces of the Cosmos. There is no longer a matter that finds its corresponding principle of intelligibility in form. It is now a question of elaborating a material charged with harnessing forces of a different order: the visual material must capture nonvisibie forces. *Render visible*, Klee said; not render or reproduce the visible. From this perspective, philosophy follows the same movement as the other activities; whereas romantic philosophy still appealed to a formal synthetic identity ensuring a continuous intelligibility of matter (a priori synthesis), modern philosophy tends to elaborate a material of thought in order to capture forces that are not thinkable in themselves. This is Cosmos philosophy, after the manner of Nietzsche. The molecular material has even become so deterritorialized that we can no longer even speak of matters of expression, as we did in romantic territoriality. *Matters of expression are superseded by a material of capture.* The forces to be captured are no longer those of the earth, which still constitute a great expressive Form, but the forces of an immaterial, nonformal, and energetic Cosmos. The painter Millet used to say that what counts in painting is not, for example, what a peasant is carrying, whether it is a sacred object or a sack of potatoes, but its exact weight. This is the postromantic turning point: the essential thing is no longer forms and matters, or themes, but forces, densities, intensities. The earth itself swings over, tending to take on the value of pure material for a force of gravitation or weight. Perhaps it is not until Cezanne that rocks begin to exist uniquely through the forces of folding they harness, landscapes through thermal and magnetic forces, and apples through forces of germination: nonvisual forces that nevertheless have been rendered visible. When forces become necessarily cosmic, material becomes necessarily molecular, with enormous force operating in an infinitesimal space. The problem is no longer that of the beginning, any more than it is that of a foundation-ground. It is now a problem of consistency or consolidation: how to consolidate the material, make it consistent, so that it can harness unthinkable, invisible, nonsonorous forces. Debussy ... Music molecularizes sound matter and in so doing becomes capable of harnessing nonsonorous forces such as Duration and Intensity. (51) *Render Duration sonorous.* Let us recall Nietzsche's idea of the eternal return as a little ditty, a refrain, but which captures the mute and unthinkable forces of the Cosmos. We thus leave behind the assemblages to enter the age of the Machine, the immense mechanosphere, the plane of cosmicization of forces to be harnessed. Varèse's procedure, at the dawn of this age, is exemplary: a musical machine of consistency, a sound machine (not a machine for reproducing sounds), which molecularizes and atomizes, ionizes sound matter, and harnesses a cosmic energy. (52) If this machine must have an assemblage, it is the synthesizer. By assembling modules, source elements, and elements for treating sound (oscillators, generators, and transformers), by arranging microintervals, the synthesizer makes audible the sound process itself, the production of that process, and puts us in contact with still other elements beyond sound matter. (53) It unites disparate elements in the material, and transposes the parameters from one formula to another. The synthesizer, with its operation of consistency, has taken the place of the ground in a priori synthetic judgment: its synthesis is of the molecular and the cosmic, material and force, not form and matter, *Grund* and territory. Philosophy is no longer synthetic judgment; it is like a thought synthesizer functioning to make thought travel, make it mobile, make it a force of the Cosmos (in the same way as one makes sound travel).

This synthesis of disparate elements is not without ambiguity. It has the same ambiguity, perhaps, as the modern valorization of children's drawings, texts by the mad, and concerts of noise. Sometimes one overdoes it, puts too much in, works with a jumble of lines and sounds; then instead of producing a cosmic machine capable of "rendering sonorous," one lapses back to a machine of reproduction that ends up reproducing nothing but a scribble effacing all lines, a scramble effacing all sounds. The claim is that one is opening music to all events, all irruptions, but one ends up reproducing a scrambling that prevents any event from happening. All one has left is a resonance chamber well on the way to forming a black hole. A material that is too rich remains too "territorialized": on noise sources, on the nature of the objects ... (this even applies to Cage's prepared piano). One makes an aggregate fuzzy, instead of defining the fuzzy aggregate by the operations of consistency or consolidation pertaining to it. For this is the essential thing: *a fuzzy aggregate, a synthesis of disparate elements, is defined only by a degree of consistency that makes it possible to distinguish the disparate elements constituting that aggregate (discernibility).* (54)   The material must be sufficiently deterritorialized to be molecularized and open onto something cosmic, instead of lapsing into a statistical heap. This condition is met only if there is a certain simplicity in the nonuniform material: a maximum of calculated sobriety in relation to the disparate elements and the parameters. The sobriety of the assemblages is what makes for the richness of the Machine's effects. People often have too much of a tendency to reterritorialize on the child, the mad, noise. If this is done, one *fuzzifies* instead of making the fuzzy aggregate consist, or harnessing cosmic forces in the deterritorialized material. That is why it infuriated Paul Klee when people would talk about the "childishness" of his drawings (and Varèse when they would talk about sound effects, etc.). According to Klee, what is needed in order to "render visible" or harness the Cosmos is a pure and simple line accompanied by the idea of an object, and nothing more: if you multiply the lines and take the whole object, you get nothing but a scramble, and visual sound effects. (55) According to Varèse, in order for the projection to yield a highly complex form, in other words, a cosmic distribution, what is necessary is a simple figure in motion and a plane that is itself mobile; otherwise, you get sound effects. Sobriety, sobriety: that is the common prerequisite for the deterritorialization of matters, the molecularization of material, and the cosmicization of forces. Maybe a child can do that. But the sobriety involved is the sobriety of a becoming-child that is not necessarily the becoming *of* the child, quite the contrary; the becoming-mad involved is not necessarily the becoming *of* the madman, quite the contrary. It is clear that what is necessary to make sound travel, and to travel around sound, is very pure and simple sound, an emission or wave without harmonics (La Monte Young has been successful at this). The more rarefied the atmosphere, the more disparate the elements you will find. Your synthesis of disparate elements will be all the *stronger* if you proceed with a sober gesture, an act of consistency, capture, or extraction that works in a material that is not meager but prodigiously simplified, creatively limited, selected. For there is no imagination outside of technique. The modern figure is not the child or the lunatic, still less the artist, but the cosmic artisan: a homemade atomic bomb-it's very simple really, it's been proven, it's been done. To be an artisan and no longer an artist, creator, or founder, is the only way to become cosmic, to leave the milieus and the earth behind. The invocation to the Cosmos does not at all operate as a metaphor; on the contrary, the operation is an effective one, from the moment the artist connects a material with forces of consistency or consolidation.

Material thus has three principal characteristics: it is a molecularized matter; it has a relation to forces to be harnessed; and it is defined by the operations of consistency applied to it. Finally, it is clear that the relation to the earth and the people has changed, and is no longer of the romantic type. The earth is now at its most deterritorialized: not only a point in a galaxy, but one galaxy among others. The people is now at its most molecularized: a molecular population, a people of oscillators as so many forces of interaction. The artist discards romantic figures, relinquishes both the forces of the earth and those of the people. The combat, if combat there is, has moved. The established powers have occupied the earth, they have built people's organizations. The mass media, the great people's organizations of the party or union type, are machines for reproduction, fuzzification machines that effectively scramble all the terrestrial forces of the people. The established powers have placed us in the situation of a combat at once atomic and cosmic, galactic. Many artists became aware of this situation long ago, even before it had been installed (Nietzsche, for example). They became aware of it because the same vector was traversing their own domain: a molecularization, an atomization of the material, coupled with a cosmicization of the forces taken up by that material. The question then became whether molecular or atomic "populations" of all natures (mass media, monitoring procedures, computers, space weapons) would continue to bombard the existing people in order to train it or control it or annihilate it-or if other molecular populations were possible, could slip into the first and give rise to a people yet to come. As Virilio says in his very rigorous analysis of the depopulation of the peopie and the deterritorialization of the earth, the question has become: „To dwell as a poet or as an assassin?" (56) The assassin is one who bombards the existing people with molecular populations that are forever closing all of the assemblages, hurling them into an ever wider and deeper black hole. The poet, on the other hand, is one who lets loose molecular populations in hopes that this will sow the seeds of, or even engender, the people to come, that these populations will pass into a people to come, open a cosmos. Once again, we must not make it seem as though the poet gorged on metaphors: it may be that the sound molecules of pop music are at this very moment implanting here and there a people of a new type, singularly indifferent to the orders of the radio, to computer safeguards, to the threat of the atomic bomb. In this respect, the relation of artists to the people has changed significantly: the artist has ceased to be the One-Alone withdrawn into him- or herself, but has also ceased to address the people, to invoke the people as a constituted force. Never has the artist been more in need of a people, while stating most firmly that the people is lacking-the people is what is most lacking. We are not referring to popular or populist artists. Mallarmé said that the Book needed a people. Kafka said that literature is the affair of the people. Klee said that the people is essential *yet lacking*. Thus the problem of the artist is that the modern depopulation of the people results in an open earth, and by means of art, or by means to which art contributes. Instead of being bombarded from all sides in a limiting cosmos, the people and the earth must be like the vectors of a cosmos that carries them off; then the cosmos itself will be art. From depopulation, make a cosmic people; from deterritorialization, a cosmic earth-that is the wish of the artisan-artist, here, there, locally. Our governments deal with the molecular and the cosmic, and our arts make them their affair also, with the same stakes, the people and the earth, and with unfortunately incomparable, but nevertheless competitive, means. Is it not of the nature of creations to operate in silence, locally, to seek consolidation everywhere, to go from the molecular to an uncertain cosmos, whereas the processes of destruction and conservation work in bulk, take center stage, occupy the entire cosmos in order to enslave the molecular and to stick it in a conservatory or a bomb?

These three "ages," the classical, romantic, and modern (for lack of a better term), should not be interpreted as an evolution, or as structures separated by signifying breaks. They are assemblages enveloping different Machines, or different relations to the Machine. In a sense, everything we attribute to an age was already present in the preceding age. Forces, for example: it has always been a question of forces, designated either as forces of chaos or forces of the earth. Similarly, for all of time painting has had the project of rendering visible, instead of reproducing the visible, and music of rendering sonorous, instead of reproducing the sonorous. Fuzzy aggregates have been constituting themselves and inventing their processes of consolidation all along. A *freeing of the molecular* was already found in classical matters of content, operating by destratification, and in romantic matters of expression, operating by decoding. The most we can say is that when forces appear as forces of the earth or of chaos, they are not grasped directly as forces but as reflected in relations between matter and form. Thus it is more a question of thresholds of perception, or thresholds of discernibility belonging to given assemblages. It is only after matter has been sufficiently deterritorialized that it itself emerges as molecular and brings forth pure forces attributable only to the Cosmos. It had been present "for all of time," but under different perceptual conditions. New conditions were necessary for what was buried or covered, inferred or concluded, presently to rise to the surface. What was, composed in an assemblage, what was still only composed, becomes a component of a new assemblage. In this sense, all history is really the history of perception, and what we make history with is the matter of a becoming, not the subject matter of a story. Becoming is like the machine: present in a different way in every assemblage, passing from one to the other, opening one onto the other, outside any fixed order or determined sequence.

We are now ready to return to the refrain. We can propose a new classification system: milieu refrains, with at least two parts, one of which answers the other (the piano and the violin); natal refrains, refrains of the territory, where the part is related to the whole, to an immense refrain of the earth, according to relations that are themselves variable and mark in each instance the disjunction between the earth and the territory (the lullaby, the drinking song, hunting song, work song, military song, etc.); folk and popular refrains, themselves tied to an immense song of the people, according to variable relations of crowd individuations that simultaneously bring into play affects and nations (the Polish, Auvergnat, German, Magyar, or Romanian, but also the Pathetic, Panicked, Vengeful, etc.); molecularized refrains (the sea and the wind) tied to cosmic forces, the Cosmos refrain. For the Cosmos itself is a refrain, and the ear also (everything that has been taken for a labyrinth is in fact a refrain). But precisely why is the refrain eminently sonorous? Why this privileging of the ear, when even animals and birds present us with so many visual, chromatic, postural, and gestural refrains? Does the painter have fewer refrains than the musician? Are there fewer refrains in Cézanne or Klee than in Mozart, Schumann, or Debussy? Taking Proust's examples: Does Vermeer's little yellow span of wall, or a painter's flowers, Elstir's roses, constitute less of a refrain than Vinteuil's little phrase? There is surely no question here of declaring a given art supreme on the basis of a formal hierarchy of absolute criteria. Our problem is more modest: comparing the powers or coefficients of deterritorialization of sonorous and visual components. It seems that when sound deterritorializes, it becomes more and more refined; it becomes specialized and autonomous. Color clings more, not necessarily to the object, but to territoriality. When it deterritorializes, it tends to dissolve, to let itself be steered by other components. This is evident in phenomena of synesthesia, which are not reducible to a simple color-sound correspondence; sounds have a piloting role and induce colors that *are superposed* upon the colors we see, lending them a properly sonorous rhythm and movement. (57) Sound owes this power not to signifying or "communicational" values (which on the contrary presuppose that power), nor to physical properties (which would privilege light over sound), but to a phylogenetic line, a machinic phylum that operates in sound and makes it a cutting edge of deterritorialization. But this does not happen without great ambiguity: sound invades us, impels us, drags us, transpierces us. It takes leave of the earth, as much in order to drop us into a black hole as to open us up to a cosmos. It makes us want to die. Since its force of deterritorialization is the strongest, it also effects the most massive of reterritorializations, the most numbing, the most redundant. Ecstasy and hypnosis. Colors do not move a people. Flags can do nothing without trumpets. Lasers are modulated on sound. The refrain is sonorous par excellence, but it can as easily develop its force into a sickly sweet ditty as into the purest motif, or Vinteuil's little phrase. And sometimes the two combine: Beethoven used as a "signature tune." The potential fascism of music. Overall, we may say that music is plugged into a machinic phylum infinitely more powerful than that of painting: a line of selective pressure. That is why the musician has a different relation to the people, machines, and the established powers than does the painter. In particular, the established powers feel a keen need to control the distribution of black holes and lines of deterritorialization in this phylum of sounds, in order to ward off or appropriate the effects of musical machinism. Painters, at least as commonly portrayed, may be much more open socially, much more political, and less controlled from without and within. That is because each time they paint, they must create or recreate a phylum, and they must do so on the basis of bodies of light and color they themselves produce, whereas musicians have at their disposal a kind of germinal continuity, even if it is latent or indirect, on the basis of which they produce sound bodies. Two different movements of creation: one goes from *soma* to *germen*, and the other from *germen* to *soma*. The painter's refrain is like the flipside of the musician's, a negative of music.

So just what is a refrain? *Glass harmonica*: the refrain is a prism, a crystal of space-time. It acts upon that which surrounds it, sound or light, extracting from it various vibrations, or decompositions, projections, or transformations. The refrain also has a catalytic function: not only to increase the speed of the exchanges and reactions in that which surrounds it, but also to assure indirect interactions between elements devoid of so-called natural affinity, and thereby to form organized masses. The refrain is therefore of the crystal or protein type. The seed, or internal structure, then has two essential aspects: augmentations and diminutions, additions and withdrawals, amplifications and eliminations by unequal values, but also the presence of a retrograde motion running in both directions, as "in the side Windows of a moving streetcar." The strange retrograde motion of *Joke*. It is of the nature of the refrain to become concentrated by elimination in a very short moment, as though moving from the extremes to a center, or, on the contrary, to develop by additions, moving from a center to the extremes, and also to travel these routes in both directions. (58) The refrain fabricates time (*du temps*). The refrain is the "implied tense" (*temps*) discussed by the linguist Gustave Guillaume. The ambiguity of the refrain is more evident now: for if the retrograde motion merely forms a closed circle, if the augmentations and diminuitions are regular, proceeding, for example, by doubled or halved values, then this false spatiotemporal rigor leaves the exterior aggregate all the fuzzier; that aggregate now has only descriptive, indicative, or associative relations with the seed. It is "a worksite of inauthentic elements for the formation of impure crystals," rather than a pure crystal that harnesses cosmic forces. The refrain remains a formula evoking a character or landscape, instead of itself constituting a rhythmic character or melodic landscape. The refrain has two poles. These poles hinge not only on an intrinsic quality but also on a state of force on the part of the listener; thus the little phrase from Vinteuil's sonata is associated with Swann's love, the character of Odette, and the landscape of the Bois de Boulogne for a long time, until it turns back on itself, opens onto itself, revealing until then unheard-of potentialities, entering into other connections, setting love adrift in the direction of other assemblages. Here, Time is not an a priori form; rather, the refrain is the a priori form of time, which in each case fabricates different times [*temps*: also, "meters," "tempos"-Trans.].

It is odd how music does not eliminate the bad or mediocre refrain, or the bad usage of the refrain, but on the contrary carries it along, or uses it as a springboard. "Ah, vous dirai-je maman" ("Ah, mamma, now you shall know"), "Elle avait une jambe de bois" ("She had a wooden leg"), "Frère Jacques." Childhood or bird refrain, folk song, drinking song, Viennese waltz, cow bells: music uses anything and sweeps everything away. Not that a folk song, bird song, or children's song is reducible to the kind of closed and associative formula we just mentioned. Instead, what needs to be shown is that a musician requires a *first type* of refrain, a territorial or assemblage refrain, in order to transform it from within, deterritorialize it, producing a refrain of the *second type* as the final end of music: the cosmic refrain of a sound machine. Gisèle Brelet, discussing Bartók, gives a good formulation of the problem of the two types: beginning from popular and territorial *melodies* that are autonomous, self-sufficient, and closed in upon themselves, how can one construct a new chromaticism that places them in communication, thereby creating *"themes"* bringing about a development of Form, or rather a becoming of Forces? The problem is a general one because in many directions refrains will be planted by a new seed that brings back modes, makes those modes communicate, undoes temperament, melds major and minor, and cuts the tonal System loose, slipping through its net instead of breaking with it. (59) We may say long live Chabrier, as opposed to Schoenberg, just as Nietzsche said long live Bizet, and for the same reasons, with the same technical and musical intent. We go from modality to an untempered. widened chromaticism. We do not need to suppress tonality, we need to turn it loose. We go from assembled refrains (territorial, popular, romantic, etc.) to the great cosmic machined refrain. But the labor of creation is already under way in the first type; it is there in its entirety. Deformations destined to harness a great force are already present in the small-form refrain or rondo. Childhood scenes, children's games: the starting point is a childlike refrain, but the child has wings already, he becomes celestial. The becoming-child of the musician is coupled with a becoming-aerial of the child, in a nondecomposable block. The memory of an angel, or rather the becoming of a cosmos. Crystal: the becoming-bird of Mozart is inseparable from a becoming-initiate of the bird, and forms a block with it. (60) It is the extremely profound labor dedicated to the first type of refrain that creates the second type, or the little phrase of the Cosmos. In a concerto, Schumann requires all the assemblages of the orchestra to make the cello wander the way a light fades into the distance or is extinguished. In Schumann, a whole learned labor, at once rythmic, harmonic, and melodic, has this sober and simple result: *deterritorialize the refrain.*(61) Produce a deterritorialized refrain as the final end of music, release it in the Cosmos-that is more important than building a new system. Opening the assemblage onto a cosmic force. In the passage from one to the other, from the assemblage of sounds to the Machine that renders it sonorous, from the becoming-child of the musician to the becoming-cosmic of the child, many dangers crop up: black holes, closures, paralysis of the finger and auditory hallucinations, Schumann's madness, cosmic force gone bad, a note that pursues you, a sound that transfixes you. Yet one was already present in the other; the cosmic force was already present in the material, the great refrain in the little refrains, the great maneuver in the little maneuver. Except we can never be sure we will be strong enough, for we have no system, only lines and movements. Schumann.

Notes

(51) In his book on Debussy, Barraqué analyzes the «dialogue of the wind and the sea" in terms of forces instead of themes: pp. 153-154. See Messiaen's statements on his own works: sounds are no longer anything more "than vulgar means of expression intended to make durations measurable."

(52) Odile Vivier describes Varèse's procedures for treating sound matter, in:*Varèse* (Paris: Seuil, 1973: the use of pure sounds actinf as a prism (p 36); mechanisms of projection on to a plane (pp. 45 and 50); non-octave-forming scales (p. 75); the "ionization" procedure (pp. 98ff.); the theme of sound *molecules*, the transformations of which are determined by forces or energies (*passim*).

(53) See the interview with Stockhausen on the role of synthesizers and the effectively "cosmic" dimension of music, in *Le Monde*, July 21, 1977:

"Work with very limited materials and integrate the universe into them through a continuous variation." Richard Pinhas has written an excellent analysis of the possibilities of synthesizers in this regard, in relation to pop music: "Input, Output," in *Atem*, no. 10 (1977).

(54)   The definition of fuzzy aggregates brings up all kinds of problems because one cannot appeal to a local determination: "The set of all objects on this table" is obviously not a fuzzy set. Mathematicans concerned with the question speak only of "fuzzy subsets" because the reference set must always be an ordinary set. See Arnold Kaufmann, *Introduction to the Theory of Fuzzy Subsets*, foreward L. A. Zadeh, trans. D. L. Swanson (New York: Academic Press, 1975), and Hourya Sinacoeur, "Logique et mathématique du flou," *Critique*. no. 372 (May 1978), pp. 512-525. In considering fuzziness as the characteristic of certain sets, our point of departure was a functional, as opposed to a local, definition: sets of heterogeneous elements that have a territorial, or rather territorializing, function. But this is a nominal definition that does not take "what happened" into account. The real definition can come only at the level of processes affecting the fuzzy set; a set is fuzzy if its elements belong to it only by virtue of specific operations of consistency and consolidation, which themselves follow a special logic.

(55)   Paul Klee, *On Modern Art*, p. 53: "The legend of the childishness of my drawing must have originated from those linear compositions of mine in which I tried to combine a concrete image, say that of a man, with the pure representation of the linear element. Had I wished to present man 'as he is' then I should have had to use such a bewildering confusion of lines that pure elementary representation would have been out of the question. The result would have been vagueness beyond recognition."

(56)   Paul Virilio, *L'insiécurité du territoire* (Paris: Stock, 1975), p. 49. Henry Miller develops this theme in *The Time of the Assassins. A Study of Rimbaud* (Norfolk, Conn.: J. Laughlin, 1956), and in the text he wrote for Varèse, "Lost! Savedl" (*The Air-Conditioned Nightmare* [New York: New

Directions, 1945]). It is undoubtedly Miller who has taken the modern figure of the writer as cosmic artisan the farthest, particularly in *Sexus*.

(57) On the relation of colors to sound, see Messiaen and Samuel, *Conversations*, pp. 15-17. Messiaen faults drug users for oversimplifying the relation, which they make into a relation between a noise and a color, instead of isolating complexes of sounds-durations and complexes of colors.

(58) On the crystal, or the crystalline type, added and subtracted values, retrograde motion, see also Messiaen's texts in Samuel, *Conversations*, and those of Paul Klee in his diary, *The Diaries of Paul Klee*. 1898-1918, ed. and intro. Felix Klee (Berkeley: University of California Press, 1964).

(59) See Roland-Manuel's article, "L'évolution de l'harmonie en France et le renouveau de 1880" (pp. 867-879), and the article by Delage on Chabrier (pp. 831-840), in *Histoire de la musique*, vol. 2. And especially, Brelet's article on Bartók: "Are not the difficulties learned music experiences in utilizing popular music due to this antinomy between melody and theme? Popular music is melody, in its fullest sense, melody persuading us that it is selfsufficient and is in fact synonymous with music itself. How could it not refuse to bend to the learned development of a musical work pursuing its own ends? Many symphonies inspired by folklore are only symphonies about a popular theme, to which the learned development remains alien and exterior. The popular melody could never constitute a true theme; and that is why, in popular music, the melody is the entire work, and why once it is over it has no other resource than to repeat itself. But can't the melody transform itself into a theme? Bartók solves this problem, which was thought insoluble" (p. 1056).

(60) Marcel More, *Le dieu Mozart et le monde des oiseaux* (Paris: Gallimard, 1971), p. 168. And, on the crystal, pp. 83-89.

(61) See Alban Berg's famous analysis of "Réverie" in *Ecrits* (Paris: Ed. du Rocher, 1957), pp. 44-64.

Selected Bibliography

Adorno, Theodor W. "The Radio Symphony", originally published in 1941. Translated by Susan H. Gillespie and Richard Leppert. In: Theodor W. Adorno, *Essays on Music*. Edited by Richard Leppert. University of California Press.

Adorno, Theodor W. *Philosophy of New Music*, originally published in 1949. Translated and edited by Robert Hullot-Kentor. University of Minnesota Press.

Barthes, Roland. *Image – Music – Text*, Essays selected and translated by Stephen Head. New York 1978.

Benjamin, Walter. "The Work of Art in the Age of Mechanical Reproduction", originally published in 1936. Translated by Harry Zorn. In: *Walter Benjamin, Illuminations*, ed. by Hannah Arendt. Schocken Books, New York.

Cage, John. *Silence*. Middletown, Conneticut 1961.

Cage, John. *Empty Words*. Middletown, Conneticut 1978.

Cook, Nicholas. *Analysing Musical Multimedia*. Oxford University Press 1998.

Cox, Christoph and Warner, Daniel (eds.). *Audio Culture – Readings in Modern Music*. London and New York 2004.

Deleuze, Gilles and, Guattari, Felix. *A Thousand Plateaus: Capitalism and Schizophrenia*, translated by Brian Massumi, University of Minnesota Press 1993.

Deleuze, Gilles. *The Fold: Leibnitz and the Baroque*, translated by Tom Conley, University of Minnesota Press 1992.

Deleuze, Gilles. *Difference and Repetition.* Translated by Paul Patton. Columbia University Press 1995.

Eco, Umberto. *The Open Work.* Translated by Anna Cancogni. Harvard University Press 1989.

Eisler, Hans (and Adorno, Theodor W.). *Composing for the Films.* New York 1973.

Emmerson, Simon (ed.). *The Language of Electroacoustic Music.* London 1986.

Godlovitch, Stan. *Musical Performance.* New York, 1998.

Kittler, Friedrich. *Gramophone, Film, Typewriter.* Translated by Geoffrey Winthrop-Young and Michael Wutz. Stanford University Press 1999.

Mann, Thomas. *The Magic Mountain.* Everyman's Library 2005.

Mann, Thomas. *Doctor Faustus.* Everyman's Library 1992.

Miller, Paul D. *Rhythm Science.* mitpress 2004.

Miller, Paul D. *Sound Unbound.* mitpress 2008.

McLuhan, H. Marshall. *Understanding Media: The Extension of Man.* New York: McGraw-Hill, 1964.

Moholy-Nagy, Laszlo. "New Form in Music: Potentialities of the Phonograph." "Production – Reproduction. New Potentialities of the Phonograph." In: *Moholy-Nagy.* Edited by Krisztina Passuth, New York 1985.

Nyman, Michael. *Experimental Music,* New York 1981.

Packer, Randall and Jordan, Ken (eds.). *Multimedia – From Wagner to Virtual Reality.* New York 2001.

Perloff, Marjorie. *The Poetics of Indeterminacy: Rimbaud to Cage.* Princeton, New Jersey 1981.

Russolo, Luigi. *The Art of Noises.* Translated by Barclay Brown. New York 1986.

Sabaneev, Leonid: "Scriabins Prometheus", in: Wassily Kandinsky and Franz Marc (eds.), *The Blaue Reiter Alamanc,* ed. Klaus Lankheit and trans. Henning Falkenstein. London 1974.

Schafer, R. Murray. *The Tuning of the World.* New York 1977.

Schaeffer, Pierre. *La musique concrète,* Paris: Presses Universitaires de France, 1967, 2nd ed. 1973.

Schirmacher, Wolfgang. *Technik und Gelassenheit: Zeitkritik nach Heidegger.* Freiburg 1983.

Schmidt, Michael. "Hören mit Schmerzen - Musik vor und nach der Katastrophe." In: *Zeitkritik nach Heidegger,* ed. Wolfgang Schirmacher. Essen 1989.

Schmidt, Michael. "Hören aus der Stille." In: *Schopenhauer und die Postmoderne,* ed. Wolfgang Schirmacher. Wien 1989.

Schmidt, Michael. "Von der Interpretation zur Simulation." In: Üben und Musizieren, 12. Jahrgang/Heft 4. Mainz 1995.

Schmidt, Michael. "Die Pornographie der Schönen Stellen - Vom Verschwinden klassischer Musik in den Medien." In: Neue Musikzeitung, 44. Jahrgang/Heft 3, Regensburg 1995.

Schmidt, Michael. "Musik in den Medien: Füllhorn oder Klangtapete?" In: Frankfurter Hefte, 44. Jahrgang/Heft 11, Bonn 1997.

Schopenhauer, Arthur. *Philosophical Writings*. Edited by Wolfgang Schirmacher. Continuum International Publishing Group 1994.

Shusterman, Richard. *Pragmatist Aesthetics: Living Beauty, Rethinking Art.* Rowman and Littlefield Publishers 2000.

Stockhausen, Karlheinz. "The concept of unity in Electronic Music". In: "Perspectives of new Music", 1962, reprinted in B. Boretz and E. Cone, "Perspectives on Contemporary Music Theory". New York 1972.

Stockhausen, Karlheinz. "Four Criteria of Electronic Music." In: *Stockhausen on Music*, ed. by R. Maconie, London 1989.

Varese, Edgar. "The Liberation of Sound." In: *Contemporary Composers on Contemporary Music*. Edited by Elliott Schwartz and Barney Childs, New York 1998.

Wagner, Richard. *The Artwork of the Future*, originally published in 1849. Translation by William Ashton Ellis, University of Nebraska Press, Lincoln and London.

—— *books available from Atropos Press*

Teletheory. Gregory L. Ulmer

Philosophy of Culture-Kulturphilosophie: Schopenhauer and Tradition. Edited by Wolfgang Schirmacher.

Grey Ecology. Paul Virilio
Edited with introduction by Hubertus von Amelunxen. Translated by Drew Burk

Talking Cheddo: Liberating PanAfrikanism. Menkowra Manga Clem Marshall

The Tupperware Blitzkrieg. Anthony Metivier

Che Guevara and the Economic Debate in Cuba. Luiz Bernardo Pericás

Follow Us or Die. Vincent W.J. van Gerven Oei and Jonas Staal

Just Living: Philosophy in Artificial Life. Collected Works Volume 1.
Wolfgang Schirmacher

—— Think Media: EGS Media Philosophy Series

Wolfgang Schirmacher, editor

The Ethics of Uncertainty: Aporetic Openings. Michael Anker

Trans/actions: Art, Film and Death. Bruce Alistair Barber

Trauma, Hysteria, Philosophy. Hannes Charen and Sarah Kamens

Literature as Pure Mediality: Kafka and the Scene of Writing.
Paul DeNicola

Deleuze and the Sign. Christopher M. Drohan

Imaginality: Conversant and Eschaton. A. Staley Groves

Hospitality in the age of media representation. by Christian Hänggi

**The Organic Organisation: freedom, creativity and
the search for fulfilment.** Nicholas Ind

Media Courage: impossible pedagogy in an artificial community.
Fred Isseks

Mirrors triptych technology: Remediation and Translation Figures.
Diana Silberman Keller

Sonic Soma: Sound, Body and the Origins of the Alphabet.
Elise Kermani

The Art of the Transpersonal Self: Transformation as Aesthetic and Energetic Practice.
Norbert Koppensteiner

Can Computers Create Art? James Morris

Propaganda of the Dead: Terrorism and Revolution. Mark Reilly.

The Novel Imagery: Aesthetic Response as Feral Laboratory. Dawan Stanford.

Community without Identity: The Ontology and Politics of Heidegger.
Tony See

www.ingramcontent.com/pod-product-compliance
Lightning Source LLC
Chambersburg PA
CBHW020246290326

41930CB00038B/414